The
Paper Doll

A Collector's Guide with Prices

Barbara Chaney Ferguson

Cover design: Jann Williams
Pictured on the front cover: Paper dolls of the 1890s—Hood Family and news
supplement baby.

745.5922
FEr

Copyright © 1982
Barbara Chaney Ferguson

ISBN 0-87069-401-4
Library of Congress Catalog
Card Number 81-71155

Published by

*Wallace-Homestead Book Company
1912 Grand Avenue
Des Moines, Iowa 50305*

This book is dedicated to the memory of my mother who began my paper doll collection, to . . .

The late Maxine Waldron who so generously left her magnificent paper doll collection to the Henry Francis du Pont Winterthur Museum for all paper doll lovers to study, and to . . .

Herbert Hosmer, who created the John Greene Chandler Memorial Museum in South Lancaster, Massachusetts, for all paper doll lovers to enjoy.

Acknowledgments

There is no more important section of a book than this, for it allows me to thank the many people who made this book possible.

For their generosity, contributions, encouragement, efforts, and special knowledge, I gratefully thank collectors Betsy Addison, Cynthia Musser, Barbara Faber, Edna Corbett, and Mary Young. For the same reasons I also thank Herbert Hosmer of the Chandler Museum, Dean Keller of the Kent State Library, Dr. Frank Sommers and the staff of the Winterthur Museum, Nancy Baird of Kentucky Library, Olivia Mahoney of the Chicago Historical Society, Mary Jane Teeters-Eichacker of the Children's Museum of Indianapolis, Isabelle Silverman of the Cooper-Hewitt, Elaine Bonney of the Essex Institute, Mary Janaky of Whitman Publishing, Mrs. Edith Lowe of Samuel Lowe, and Jean Woodcock of Merrill Publishing.

I thank Herb, Vicky, Dorothy, and Kurt for photographic expertise and enthusiasm. I thank Avis Gardiner for special finds. I thank Marilyn Forney for her hospitality and the observations that led to the adventure of this book. I thank Jo Hayes for beginning my fun. Of course, as always, I thank my husband and children Nancy, Leslie, Bob, and Ed for their cheerful support, stamina, encouragement, and great gift of time.

Contents

Illustrations

The Paper Doll

Findable, affordable, makeable, collectible—paper dolls have been so treasured and cherished that many that are over one hundred years old still survive, smiling quaintly, complete with costumes, hats, and child-scrawled names.

When in the forties, Frank Sinatra crooned, ''I'm gonna buy a paper doll to call my own,'' he sang more than a ''mouthful.'' Although research and cataloging have begun, no one knows the exact paper doll population. Surprise paper dolls, manufactured or handmade, consistently emerge from the recesses of the past, not only to thrill collectors, but also to tell us something about their original decades.

From Jenny Lind to Bing Crosby, from Napoleon to Golda Meir, from Tom Thumb to the ''Fonz,'' paper dolls portray the popular period: celebrities, politicians, fashions, art styles, and even entertainments and occupations. Paper dolls, like Egyptian pharaohs, graphically bring to their afterlives their most beloved and indispensable objects.

Paper dolls wheel Columbia bicycles; they drive Model Ts; they carry canoe paddles; they use Enameline Stove Polish; and in so doing, they transcend their ephemeral origins as charming, fun paper toys, a child's momentary ''parlor amusement,'' and become significant personages, representatives of their own time, interesting, increasingly valuable, and definitely worthy of serious consideration by collectors, historians, and art lovers.

We paper doll collectors consider our paper dolls to be Americana, ephemera, folk art, pop art, and pop culture. We especially consider paper dolls fun; and in this book I wish to share with you, fellow collector or new enthusiast, the fascination of a paper doll collection from the antique through nostalgia to now.

The Boston Herald Lady.

Collectible, Findable, Affordable, Makeable

Sold in fancy gilt-edged boxes, embellished envelopes, lithographed sheets, cutout books, family magazines, fashion periodicals, newspapers, comics, greeting cards, even cereal boxes, paper dolls have appeared in such infinite variety that there is a collecting specialty suited to the taste and purse of each paper doll enthusiast.

In fact, paper dolls are so varied that no collector could possibly gather all. Some choices must be made. Cut or uncut? This is the first decision. Should one collect only the quaint antique or nostalgic charmers? A select paper doll in an antique frame is a true treasure and delight. Or perhaps a parade of celebrities would be most pleasing.

There are also endless collection combinations. Consider: Maude Adams to Rock Hudson; celebrities; sports or space; babies; brides or ballerinas; nursery story or fairytale dolls; advertising or comic book characters; the dolls of a favorite publisher (Raphael Tuck, McLoughlin, Merrill); the creations of a favorite artist (Queen Holden, Shelia Young, Grace Drayton); representatives of a favorite historical period (the gay nineties, the stylish thirties, the glamorous forties, the wild sixties); Barbies, Betsys, or Letties; handmades—the list is endless. For most of us the choice is influenced by availability and price.

Whatever your choice, however, you must not overlook the present. Contemporary paper dolls are exciting. Independent

Shaker Salt Queen in an antique frame.

Contemporary paper dolls are exciting! Model from Erte Fashion Paper Dolls of the Twenties *rendered by Susan Johnston; Nijinsky from* Nijinsky *and Pavlova by Tom Tierney.*

Erte dolls©Dover Publications, Inc., courtesy Sevenarts, Ltd., London.
Nijinsky and Pavlova©Dover Publications, Inc.

12

Bride and groom, 1890 news supplement.

artists and publishers like Dover, Merrimac, Bellerophon, and Whitman are reacting to current paper doll interest and increasing production of magnificent reproductions of older dolls and exceptionally beautiful, original new dolls. Assuredly, today's dolls will be our descendants' prizes.

In the thirties, my mother began my collection by purchasing from the five-and-dime two copies of today's highly sought movie star paper doll books. One set was for me to cut; the other was for us to save.

Lucky me! My mother had a sense of history and incredible foresight. She also loved paper dolls. She did not imagine, however, that the uncut celebrity sets bought for a dime could be worth from forty to sixty to over one hundred dollars today.

Obviously I was fortunate, and over the years, we continued the practice of purchasing two sets at a time, through the childhoods of my daughters on to just Mother and me giving each other Twiggy for Christmas.

We did well. We could have done better! We should have purchased at least four sets of our special favorites: one to cut, one to save, one to trade, and one to sell. I pass on this recommendation to you. Buy four of your contemporary favorites at a time and tuck them away. You will not regret the investment. The price will never be better, and the condition is mint!

As you noticed, I recommend that three of the four sets be preserved uncut, which brings us to an important decision for a collector, "Should dolls be collected cut or uncut?"

Uncut paper dolls are considered the most valuable by collectors. They are the most expensive, usually double the price of a complete cut set. They are most highly prized because, obviously, they are whole and in mint condition. They are also the most difficult to find.

Since paper dolls are toys and intended for play, it is only logical that the dolls surviving childhood have been cut out and played with. Many are bent, marred, or missing arms or legs. Most have lost a wardrobe piece or two. The original envelope, box, or cover has probably disappeared.

Still, collecting cut dolls has many advantages, and many collectors prefer to collect them. Some advantages are obvious: cut dolls are less expensive; far easier to obtain than uncut dolls; and also easy to display and keep. A cut doll frames well against interesting backgrounds and fits easily into photo albums for handy viewing and keeping. (See Appendix C.)

Many collectors prefer cut dolls for emotional reasons. They are collecting for their own pleasure, savoring childhood memories. Though not all collectors will admit it, it is fun to play with cut dolls, trying on hats and dresses again. Uncut dolls can be frustrating; they never don the magnificent beruffled ball gown drawn next to them. But a cut doll has clearly "lived." She has an aura of "loved" and, very often, even a name. I own an Arabella, a Nellie, a Flossie, a George Fortune and, my very favorite, Estrella Beauharness.

You will solve the cut or uncut dilemma for yourself, probably by availability and price.

So many people say, "But I never see paper dolls. I think all the sources have dried up. Where do you find them?" Finding paper dolls *is* a challenge. The supply does seem at times to have vanished. There are many more collectors now than previously. Nevertheless, as soon as one becomes discouraged, treasures appear.

There are, however, secrets.

If your prime collection interest is in antique or nostalgic dolls, find antique dealers whose taste you trust and tell them your heart's desire. They will often buy especially for you. Searching is their business, and they have sources that sometimes seem like magic. Attending antique shows very early may also help you discover dolls—or new dealers who will search for you.

Garage sales and flea markets are excellent spots to find dolls from the fifties to the present. Thrift stores sometimes have a doll or two. Never pass up old copies of women's magazines, because almost all the issues from 1910 through the 1930s contained paper dolls. You may be fortunate to find a doll still whole.

If dolls from the sixties and seventies are your choice, small-town variety stores sometimes handle remainders sold as new. Always "case" any likely store, from the drugstore to a second-hand bookshop.

Contemporary paper dolls, such as those Dover, Bellerophon, and Merrimac produce, are sold in bookstores and gift shops or may be ordered from the publishers' catalogs. (See Appendixes B and E.) Child-oriented paper dolls are still sold in chain stores, and collectors should always check the racks to see what's new. Greeting card companies often incorporate paper dolls into their wares, and paper dolls turn up in cards, wrapping paper, center-pieces, even tablecloths. All are collectible.

I've saved the best paper doll sources for last. Currently there are four paper doll newsletters: The *Paper Doll Gazette,* The *Midwest Paper Doll and Toy Quarterly, Paper Playthings* and *Matchmaker.* (See Appendix for addresses.) These newsletters not only contain interesting paper doll information, but they also carry ads from independent paper doll artists and dealer-collectors who mail lists for mail-order purchase of paper dolls.

Best of all, the newsletters advertise paper doll conventions and parties that are held in varying locations. The conventions, besides presenting interesting programs, holding workshops, and attracting a delightfully congenial group, provide salesrooms for paper doll dealer-collectors, who appear like genies with boxes of fantastic dolls to sell. A convention is mecca to a collector, and I urge all who are serious to not only subscribe to the newsletters, but also to enjoy a convention.

The relative monetary value of cut and uncut dolls has already been discussed. Paper doll pricing is unique. It is probably the only collectible sold in pieces and parts. Although many collectors are shocked at current paper doll prices, it seems to me that compared to their sisters the real dolls and other high-quality collectibles like stamps and books, paper dolls are an enormous value.

The price spectrum is wide. Wonderful dolls may be purchased for dimes as well as dollars. For example, in 1981 a mint condition, rare, boxed European 1850 paper doll, Bertha in Crinoline, sold at auction for $1,000. The same year, a Raphael Tuck Artistic Doll with three dresses and three hats sold for $25; a Lion Coffee Tom Thumb advertising doll sold for $5; an uncut 1936 Winnie Winkle comic cutout sold for $15; and a 1960 Betsy McCall sold for $3. As you can see, there are dolls for every purse.

With the exception of the early antique paper dolls (which are rarely sold and usually at auction), and of the handmade dolls (which involve subjective pricing), a market estimate is given with each doll illustrated in this book. The figure quoted is for a doll in *mint* condition, i.e., in good shape and complete with costumes, hats, boxes, or envelopes. This figure is intended as a guide to buying only. Prices always vary by dealer, location, and current demand. The prices given are composite averages compiled from price lists, antique shows, flea markets, and auctions.

I've saved my favorite soap-box topic for the end. Besides being collectible, findable, and affordable, paper dolls are excitingly, delightfully makeable.

In fact, although I have not done a study, I am sure at least 95 percent of the paper doll collectors choose and cherish paper dolls for the artistic creativity they represent and inspire. The first paper dolls were handmade, some charmingly primitive, others artful; some drawn by children, others by adults. All are treasured, and every museum I've visited most appreciates its handmade dolls as ''folk art.'' The history of the printed, published commercial paper doll is paralleled by the history of the homemade-handmade paper doll, and both are highly prized collectibles.

Sadly, it seems to me, plastic, television, and structured time have robbed today's child of the simple, inexpensive creative joy of making paper dolls. I hope we adult collectors can revive this art by continuing the tradition of the homemade doll, creating them ourselves (primitively or skillfully—it does not matter) and passing along the fun of it to our families and friends.

I make my own paper dolls ''for descendant,'' and in this book's final chapter, be forewarned that you will be exhorted to join me if you are not already a paper doll creator. It is so easy. It is such fun. Descendants will thank you for your legacy. They are not art critics. Instead, they collect antique paper dolls—''from ancestor.''

Opposite page: Paper Dolls C. Guthrie Made for Me. *Treasured handmades from the Coke Collection.*
Photographed at Kentucky Library, Western Kentucky University.

I. From the Antique
Beginnings: Pantins, English Dolls, and Fashions

There have always been dolls as playthings. Primitive man fashioned them from twigs and stone. The Egyptians and Greeks created them from clay, wood, and ivory. The Indians formed them from cornhusks. There have not always been paper dolls. Although the ancient Chinese and Japanese used paper figures in religious ceremonies, these figures were not playthings. It took modern civilization, printing, and papermaking to give us the toy paper doll.

Pantins

For those who might consider the paper doll a saccharine girl's toy, some genealogical spice is added by the French pantin, considered the ancestor to both the puppet and the commercial toy paper doll. Twice in the eighteenth century, pantins were the rage of Paris, both in the salons of the wealthy and in the French royal court, where they were so uproariously entertaining and satirized the nobility so naughtily that they were banned by Louis XV—surely an uncommon distinction for a toy of paper!

In *Poupees Anciennes,* Claude Sezan quotes the French historian Bigarrure (1754):

> In France where dolls were more and more a fashion, still another specialty began, and people could buy them with luck at the seller of mirrors, at the spectacle shop, the haberdashers or fancy goods store.... This imaginative toy which so much amused the Grand came into vogue in 1725. The most beautiful were painted in watercolors and engraved in shapes which one put together after cutting.
>
> All Paris was mad for them, and it was not always a harmless habit. One reads, "A lady sold nearly all her wardrobe and a part of her jewels to have in her cabinet de toilette fifty of the most brilliant pantins!"*
>
> Also the most famous artists consented to design these fragile toys giving them great value, and thus the mad pursuit caught on!

Mr. Sezan also quotes the French diarist Barbier, who wrote of the year 1747:

> In style last year toys were invented called pantins first for child's play and then to amuse all.... This invention is not new, only rediscovered like many other things and twenty years ago it was the same fashion.... They are little figures made of cardboard, with limbs separate, that is to say, cut out separately and attached by strings which can make them play and twitch.... They can dance. These little figures represent Harlequin, Scaramouch, a baker's boy, a shepherd, a shepherdess, etc., and all are painted according to all sorts of fashions.... Some are painted by the best painters, among them Monsieur Boucher, the most famous of the Academy and they are very expensive. There are also some with figures too "free."

These are the trifles which occupy and amuse all Paris and one cannot find a house where they are not hanging on the mantlepiece. They are presents to both men and women and the rage this year for filling Christmas boxes.

Francois Boucher, master of the rococo style, premier painter to Louis XV and a favorite of Louis's mistress, Madame de Pompadour, was said to be the most distinguished of the pantin painters. Barbier records that the Duchess of Chartres spent 1,500 francs for a pantin painted by him.

This fashionable French fad's demise came by royal order. Max Von Boehn, in *Dolls and Puppets,* quotes the 1756 edict issued by Louis to prohibit the pantin. They were banned "because women, under the lively influence of this continual jumping, were in danger of bringing children into the world with twisted limbs like the pantins."

Eighteenth century French pantin.

Courtesy of John Greene Chandler Memorial Museum, South Lancaster, Mass.

Opposite page: Eighteenth century watercolor French pantin.

Courtesy of John Greene Chandler Memorial Museum, South Lancaster, Mass.

*Ancestress to the paper doll collector, no doubt.

Of course, the French were not the only ones who played with jointed paper dolls; other countries played with them, too. In Germany these articulated figures were called hampelmann. In the United States they were known as jumping jacks.

Pantin fever seemed to progress from France to England in the eighteenth century. There these toys were popular as parlor amusements, much to the dismay of the serious-minded. They were characterized as ''toys of idleness'' and ''frivolous indulgencies of the adult mind'' in the Oxford English Dictionary, which further noted pantin reaction:

London Magazine, 1774: ''the ridiculous folly of pantins. . . .''
Besant and Rich, 1781: ''A ridiculous fashion of paper doll in vogue as
a toy for ladies with nothing to do. . . .''

Any representative paper doll collection must surely include a specimen of this frivolous fellow, and an excellent pantin to search out would be one from Epinal, France, and the family printers, Imagerie Pellerin. Begun in 1773 by Jean Charles Pellerin, who was assisted by his brothers, this printer began by using woodblock and four stenciled colors. Their first prints were religious illustrations, followed through the years by playing cards, pantins, paper dolls and paper soldiers.

Favorite subjects for Pellerin pantins, as with ''all Paris'' in 1747 to 1756, were the beloved characters from the commedia dell'arte, a type of sixteenth century improvisational play, whose plot made use of stock characters: Harlequin, Columbine, Pierrot, Pierrette, Punchinello, abbes, and clowns. So many sheets d'Epinal were printed over the years that a patient collector might successfully search for and find such a treasure.

Pantins, jumping jacks, and hampelmanns are still popular today. Dover Publishing Company has reproduced, in *Antique French Jumping Jacks,* some of Epinal's interesting and rare pantins, and this book makes an excellent contemporary addition to any collection.

Here, however, it is important to issue a note of warning. The current interest in collecting paper dolls has caused a prolific number of paper doll reproductions from publishers. They are exceptionally well done and highly collectible in themselves. In uncut, pristine state, all the reproduced dolls are clearly labeled ''reproduction.'' Unfortunately, however, we collectors feel that through time and cutting, the origins of these dolls are likely to be obscured, and an unwary collector may well be sold, either purposely or innocently, a paper reproduction at an original price. This is already happening. Beware. In this book, known reproductions of originals will be pointed out.

Of course, the finest contemporary addition to any collection in the best parlor amusement tradition would be an original handmade pantin. Should you feel inspired, threading directions are shown.

Somewhere, probably in France, in the middle of the eighteenth century, someone created the first paper doll, a paper figure with a change of paper costume. It was probably a handmade delight and a commercial success. Most probably, the first paper doll was created by a dressmaker to show current fashion. This, however, is hypothesis. No one knows for sure, and no one can pinpoint exactly the beginnings of paper dolls.

Pantin. Epinal.

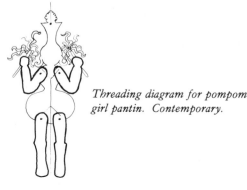

Threading diagram for pompom girl pantin. Contemporary.

Early costume, eighteenth century.
Courtesy Henry Francis du Pont Winterthur Museum, Joseph Downs Manuscript Collection/
The Maxine Waldron Collection of Children's and Paper Toys

The fact is, however, that in the early seventeenth and eighteenth centuries, fashion centers were Vienna, Berlin, and Paris. It was from France in the early eighteenth century that fashion dolls or mannequins were exported to show the latest mode. They were first sent to the German courts, then to Italy, England, and, finally, the colonies. The transition from exported fashion doll to paper doll to fashion plate was a matter of time, invention, and convenience.

From the magnificent paper doll collection of the late Maxine Waldron in the Francis du Pont Winterthur Museum comes one of the earliest known examples of paper fashion. The illustration of Mrs. Waldron's Early Costume is representative of the style of the mid-1700s. It is obviously a fashion model, made, it is presumed, for a lost paper figure. It has one paper hand. The doll's elaborate gown is 10″ tall and is made of a combination of fabric and paper. The cloth is embroidered chenille. The dress includes netting, ribbons, feathers, and is edged in gold. The complete costume is in tan, greens, orange, and red.

Also from the collection of Mrs. Maxine Waldron at Winterthur are several exquisite handmade paper booklets,

delicate works of art, which in a cutout series show the hair, ornaments, and shoulders of a lady of fashion. The artistic *Coiffures* is illustrated, c. 1786–1789.

This charming booklet is about 3″ high and is enclosed in the black case illustrated. It is an advertising brochure and includes the following:

COIFFURES
Se vend dans la meme
Chez Denis-Antoine
Rue S. Jacques—vis-a-vis
2 S. Amboise

This obviously tells the reader that the hairstyles and headdresses (it is believed both are meant by the word *coiffures*) are sold at the shop of Denis-Antoine, Saint Jacques Street, opposite 2 Saint Amboise Street.

While this booklet is not a proper paper doll, it does utilize the technique of change of costume in paper, and the whole is a true treasure. There are three quaint heads incorporated into the design of this booklet, each framed in the cutout oval, which gives each page the appearance of a watercolor miniature.

Eighteenth century Coiffures.
Tiny cutout French watercolor booklet displaying headdresses for sale.

Courtesy Henry Francis du Pont Winterthur Museum,
Joseph Downs Manuscript Collection/
The Maxine Waldron Collection of Children's and Paper Toys

19

English Dolls

In *Paper Dolls and How to Make Them* by Edith Flack Ackley, this oft-quoted notice from the 1791 *Journal des Luxus de Moden* is given:

> A new and pretty invention is the so-called English doll which we have lately received from London. It is properly a toy for little girls, but it is so tasteful that mothers and grown women will likely also want to play with it, the more since good or bad taste in dress or coiffure can be observed and, so to speak, studied. The doll is a young female figure cut of stout cardboard. It is about eight inches high, has simply curled hair, and is dressed in underclothes and corset. With it go six complete sets of tastefully designed dresses and headdresses.

The wonderful paper doll collection at the John Greene Chandler Memorial Museum in South Lancaster, Massachusetts, is illustrated. It includes an English doll dated 1790 and made in Nurnberg, Germany. Mr. Hosmer, great-nephew of John Greene Chandler and founder of the museum, also has in his own collection a female English doll, companion to the male.

Box of English Doll. Germany, 1790.
Courtesy of John Greene Chandler Memorial Museum, South Lancaster, Mass.

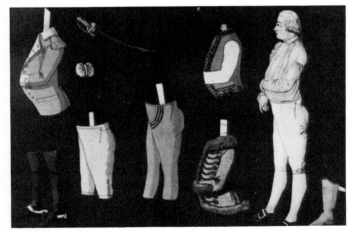

English Doll. Fashion Doll Game, German, 1790.
Courtesy of John Greene Chandler Memorial Museum, South Lancaster, Mass.

These dolls are figures contained in boxes with filelike envelopes and a paper strap holding each costume. The doll is made to lie flat, and clothes are placed on it in sections. It is obviously a predecessor to the S. & J. Fuller Protean Figure of 1810, except that these English dolls do not come with a landscape to lie upon.

Mr. Hosmer's doll contains a letter of directions written in old German script. I am indebted to Gisella Stark for this translation:

Short Directions on how to dress this doll

So as to have the cut-out so-called "English Doll" give you the pleasure you are expecting from this you must do the following: Lay it down horizontally or evenly and start at the bottom with dresses until it is completely covered. For instance, if you want to see it in *en habit de gala** you should start with the shirt and put it exactly on top of the right arm. Then you take the dress so that the skirt covers the corset and then you put the scarf on so that all is covered. Then you put on the hairdo, also two gloves with the fan, which has to be put in the hands. Now the doll is ready to parade in beautiful, fashionable costume.

With the male figure you do the same thing if you want to see it in Gallic dress. You take the pants, put them on the two thighs so that the underwear is covered, then take the rest, put on the shirt and leave the left arm exposed. Then you take the jacket and lay it over the arm. Finally put on the tie, sword, and hat so that this doll also can parade in its most beautiful fashion.

If you want each and every piece of clothing at the place where it should be, use a little glue-wax for best results.

This fashion doll game, changing the clothes, especially "socially," can give a lot of entertainment, which can also be augmented through new sets of clothing and costume to make the whole thing more interesting to more people.

*The French phrase was used in the German to mean *French dress*.

It is interesting to note that the doll is referred to as a "fashion doll game" played socially. One assumes this means in the company of friends, and that "glue-wax" might be used in attaching the clothes. In the 1880s beeswax was sometimes used to hold costumes on dolls, and one wonders if this is a similar substance.

Sultan's costume.
From page of German English Doll, 1790.
Courtesy of John Greene Chandler Memorial Museum, South Lancaster, Mass.

Fashions

Because antique paper dolls were originally cut in manufacture (toy books) or cut out by children, dolls and costumes are often found without identifying dates and marks. It is important for the collector to recognize the style and characteristics of the publishers, and it is also important to know period fashion. The following fashion information is simplified.

Feminine frippery of the 1800s.

Fortunately, women's fashion in the 1800s is easy to date. The skirt is the identifying characteristic. Skirts at both the beginning and end of the century were narrow. In midcentury (1840–1868), they were full in crinoline and hoop. Romantic short fullness was worn in the beginning decades. Hoops disappeared after the Civil War, when fullness went to the back in overskirts, flounces, puffs, bustles, and trains. In the 1890s women became "hour glasses," and by 1903, the fashionable shape was the kangaroo bend or S curve and relatively narrow skirts.

Splendid suits, as McLoughlin Brothers termed male paper doll attire in the 1800s, were really only splendid in the first decade of the century. Thereafter, they became progressively more uniform and dull. The change in male occupation was responsible for this. Society moved from the rural estates, farms, shops, crafts, to the city, and manufacturing, banking, and business took over.

The pants and coat are the identifying characteristics. In the beginning of the century, breeches (pants to the calf) were worn, and pantaloons (long pants with elastic that went under the foot)

were just appearing. Coats were double-breasted with tails, and shirts had high pointed collars to display the cravat. Tall beaver hats were the style.

Splendid suits of the 1800s.

By 1820 both trousers and pantaloons were worn. Coats became frock coats, skirted coats with nipped-in waists. From 1825 to 1830 collars were high and pointed, and stocks and cravats were an important feature of the costume. Beau Brummel, in the 1800s, set the English fashion style. He was noted for spotless linen and many methods of tying a cravat. In 1830 the paletot coat appeared for sport. This was a straight-cut coat, and eventually it became the modern suit coat and dinner jacket.

In 1850–1869, trousers were worn exclusively. The coat was the frock coat in two versions, one for day and one for evening. This coat has been called "the hallmark of Victorian respectability." In 1850 the waistcoat matched the trousers; in 1860 there were three-piece suits. Men wore Wellington boots and carried a walking stick. Shawls were the fashion for men in 1850. Lincoln is often pictured in one; the father of the Anson Randolph paper doll family wore one. Top hats were made of silk.

In 1870 the frock coat became the morning coat and was worn on special occasions. The lounge jacket (from the paletot) with a matching waistcoat became popular for informal occasions. The Norfolk jacket, a straight jacket with a belt and pleat in back, was also popular and remained so through the 1900s. Bowlers or derbies appeared, although the top hat was worn the most by the prosperous businessman.

In 1880 the bottom of the trouser was turned up. By 1890 there was a crease down the center of the pantleg. Lounge jackets were also boating jackets, and straw boaters (hats) and knickerbockers were worn with Norfolk jackets for sport.

By 1900 a gentleman's wardrobe consisted of black, gray, or drab morning coat, striped trousers, butterfly collar, spats, cane, top hat, and silk cravat. He owned a lounge suit of tweed or stripe and a derby hat. In summer he wore a boating jacket and white flannel trousers. With them he wore a boater or panama (straw) hat and buckskin shoes. In winter he needed a smoking jacket, and for motoring he needed a Norfolk jacket, knickerbockers, dust coat, motoring cap, and goggles.

Children's fashion in the 1800s emulated the adult styles. Little girls wore shorter versions of their mothers' dresses. Little boys were dressed like girls for the first three years of their lives.

From 1800 to 1820 little girls wore high-waisted Empire style dresses with colored sashes. There were some concessions for play, and in the 1820s pantalettes, lacy white tubes that tied around the leg, were worn. Little boys wore breeches at first and then pantaloons with elastic under the foot. These were worn with short jackets and ruffled blouses. Hats with ribbons were favored.

From 1840 to 1865 girls wore crinolines as their mothers did, and hoops when they appeared. Skirts were shorter than were the skirts of an adult and pantalettes, now drawers, were worn. Both boys and girls wore striped stockings. Indoor shoes were flat slippers with inner straps. High-button boots were worn outside. Pinafores became popular.

Tunics, belted and unbelted, knickerbockers, trousers, and short jackets were popular for boys. During this period the Scotch kilt appeared as a young man's favorite. Kilts became popular when Queen Victoria adapted them for her young sons after a visit to Balmoral. Kilts are often seen in paper dolls.

From 1869 to 1890 girls' styles included the bustle, as did mama's. The skirts were shorter. The youthful bustle was either a "polonaise" overskirt pulled back or a long "basque" bodice, a low waist tied with a large sash and with ruffles pulled to the back. High-button boots and stockings completed the costume. In the late 1870s and 1880s, Kate Greenaway's illustrations popularized a return to the Empire style of dress, and that became fashionable for special occasions. Little girls continued to wear the practical pinafore and apron.

Boys in this period wore tunics, knickerbockers, Norfolk jackets, and middy suits with sailor hats. Older boys dressed like their fathers. In the 1880s Frances Hodgson Burnett wrote *Little Lord Fauntleroy,* and black velvet ruffled suits were inflicted upon young boys.

In the 1890s skirts, shirtwaists, leg-of-mutton sleeves, wide collars, pinafores, and high-button boots were worn by girls. Boys' styles remained about the same.

Little folks' fashion of the 1800s.

Toy Books

In 1810 charming small chapbooks, called toy books, emerged in England, produced by S. & J. Fuller, The Temple of Fancy, Rathbone Place, London, where "also were sold books of Instruction In Landscapes, Flowers and Figures, and every requisite used in Drawing."

As advertised in 1810 on the envelope of the toy book *Little Fanny,* this establishment also sold:

> A new Essay of Flower Painting by Edward Pretty. Where also may be had the greatest Variety of Fancy Articles Fire Screens, Card, Racks . . . Workboxes and Baskets and every description of fancy embossed gold borders, Papers and Medallions for useful and Polite Amusement.

The toy books told a morality tale "exemplified in a series of figures that drefs and undrefs." They were immensely popular and went into numerous printings.

The United States was still a young nation in 1810. James Madison was president. Our population totaled 7,049,000. Napoleon waged war in Europe, and we were unable to remain neutral. Protecting our ships and seamen from the British, we fought the War of 1812. The war lasted until 1814 when commerce with Great Britain recommenced. It is certain that with peace came many merchant ships in whose holds were stowed little English toy books for the edification and joy of fortunate American children.

There were no foreign copyright laws in the 1800s, and toy books were so popular that two American printers copied them from 1812 to 1820. J. Belcher of Boston, Massachusetts, produced both *Little Fanny* and *Little Henry.* William Charles of Philadelphia copied *Little Fanny.* The Charles book did not contain separate cutout figures of Fanny, but the Belcher book did.

A showcase in the wonderful John Greene Chandler Memorial in South Lancaster, Massachusetts, is illustrated. This case contains three versions of *Little Fanny,* a most popular Fuller toy book, which tells of Fanny, who did not wish to do her lessons, but preferred to try on her lovely new cape. A series of misadventures fall upon her, until at last she is reunited with her parents.

The lower series of figures is a handmade set of *Little Fanny;* the top series is from an English Fuller 1830 reprint of *Fanny;* and the middle series is the American Belcher *Little Fanny.*

As you can see, the versions differ. The 1810 and handmade *Little Fanny*s include all red capes; the 1830 reprint is updated to a green cape. Both the Belcher and 1830 sets are most rare.

The treasure of my collection is illustrated. It is a fourth printing of a Fuller English toy book called *Ellen* or *The Naughty Girl Reclaimed.* Ellen's action costume wardrobe is 171 years old, but complete even to the dunce cap. The book is small, 4" high, and is contained in a fancy embellished case tied with a ribbon. You can see there is no doll. Ellen's head slips neatly into a pocket glued to the back of each costume.

Fuller books are engraved, and the costume figures are hand-painted. The figures were probably hand-cut and the pockets hand-pasted. The name of the printer is included, D. M. Sury, Berwick Street, Soho.

I feel particularly fortunate to own this toy book because its heroine is a naughty, messy, rebellious child, and she is thus most congenial, familiar, and amusing. The dreadful episodic adventure that befalls Ellen as a result of her naughtiness is entertaining today, and it must surely have effectively not only preached goodness to the young of 1810, but also inspired a great terror of gypsy violinists!

Little Fanny display. Top: English S. & J. Fuller 1830 reprint of 1810 original. Center: American version by Belcher, 1812–1820. Bottom: handmade set of Little Fanny.
Courtesy of John Greene Chandler Memorial Museum, South Lancaster, Mass.

Little Ellen. S. & J. Fuller, 1810.

The figures are illustrated and with each is a wonderful verse.

Little Ellen.
Episodes I,
II, and III.

Episode I

Ellen makes her First Appearance in a White Frock, with a Book at her Feet.

This little girl, whom now you see,
To mind mamma will not agree,
And though her face is fair and mild
You view a stubborn, naughty child:
Nay, Ellen is so wayward grown,
Her book upon the ground is thrown,
And kind mamma, who loves so well,
Can neither make her read or spell:
With little sisters she will fight,
And scratch and pinch—nay, sometimes bite . . .
[Mamma resolves to] try one little plan,
Which, if it fails, she then will send
Her far from home without a friend.

Episode II

Ellen dressed in a Blue Hat and Feather . . .

[Mamma purchases a new hat and spencer to please Little
Ellen and bribe her to goodness, and Ellen]
Promises, in milder mood,
She'll now indeed be very good;
Entreats mamma to let her go
And take a walk [with curtsey low].

Episode III

Ellen appears in a deplorable condition her Frock and Spencer splashed with Mud.

Ellen in spite of promise made,
Would please herself while out she staid . . .
She'd gather every berry wild . . .
[Ellen falls into a muddy ditch] where all
Her clothes were spoil'd—unlucky fall!

Little Ellen.
Episodes IV,
V, and VI.

Episode IV

Ellen is now dressed in coloured Frock and Blue Cloak, with a Bundle in her Hand.

[Ellen is sent away to the Nurse, who keeps the village
school.]

24

Episode V

Ellen stands in a Disgraceful Situation, with the Foolscap on her Head.

The book she threw in Nurse's face,
Who on her head the foolscap plac'd.

Episode VI

Ellen appears in the Dress of a Gypsy Girl, Sitting in a Wood.

Now sadly alter'd Ellen's seen.
One day she left her [Nurse] in a pet
And rambled far, till near a wood . . .
Her cloak it caught some gypsy's eyes,
Who soon rush'd forth and seiz'd their prize . . .
[Ellen is forced to work for the cruel gypsys.]
At last too ill . . . cruel gypsys in a fright
Forsook her in this wretched plight.

Little Ellen.
Episodes VII,
VIII, and IX.

Episode VII

Ellen now makes a more pleasing appearance.

A neat old woman crossed the wood
To reach her cot that near it stood,
Rescued the child, I'm glad to tell . . .
No longer arrogant and vain,
But humbly wishing to regain
Her papa's love, poor Ellen strives,
"To mend her faults with tearful eyes . . .
Repentent of her conduct grown."

Episode VIII

Ellen in Red Cloak with Basket of Fruit in her hand.

Quite alter'd now we Ellen find . . .
[The good old dame sent her to market to sell fruit;
a carriage passes containing Mamma and Papa]
Mamma screamed out with rapture wild . . .
The door was open'd, out she sprung,
And round her neck poor Ellen clung.
[Ellen is pardoned.]

Episode IX

Ellen makes her Last Appearance sitting in a Chair With a Book in her hand.

Ellen once more appears in view,
To bid you all a kind adieu,
Her sorrow from her faults begun,
She therefore hopes those faults you'll shun . . .
No longer does she fret and tease,
But happily her time she spends,
Lov'd and esteem'd by all her friends. *Finis*

Besides *Little Ellen*, S. & J. Fuller produced many other charming toy books. Among them are *Little Fanny; Little Henry; Phoebe, the Cottage Maid; Herbert, the Cottage Boy;*

Young Albert the Roscius, from Shakespeare and Other Authors. Bottom, left to right, Othello (missing black head): Young Albert: (King Henry IV, Hamlet); Top, left to right, King Richard III, Barbarrossa, As You Like It. S. & J. Fuller, 1811.

Courtesy of John Greene Chandler Memorial Museum, South Lancaster, Mass.

Lauretta, the Little Savoyard; Frank Feignwell, His attempts to amuse his Friends at Twelfth Night; Cinderella, or The Glass Slipper; and *Young Albert Roscius.* The last is illustrated. There were also versions of these stories in Dutch, German, and French. *Petit Auguste* and *Petite Helene* were two of the French toy books.

From the collection of Herbert Hosmer and the John Greene Chandler Memorial comes *The Protean Figure* or *Metamorphic Costumes.* Its relationship to the illustrated German English doll is obvious. This rare and highly collectible paper doll is also from S. J. Fuller, England, 1811.

It is contained in an envelope-like file book, similar to that of the German English doll, and it, too, contains a series of costume pieces that lie flat on the doll. An innovation is the landscape upon which the doll was placed. It is clear that these figures were not to be played with, but to be admired.

The Protean Figure came in two sizes; one set containing ten costumes and the other, twelve. Costumes include walking dress, naval uniform, monk's habit, Turkish costume, Quaker's habit, morning suit, German hussar, full dress of the 1700s, knight in armor, officer's uniform (land forces), gentleman's evening costume, and a French uniform.

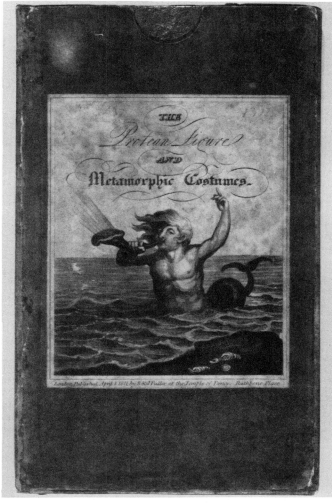

Box, The Protean Figure of Metamorphic Costume. S. & J. Fuller.

Protean Figure on landscape. S. & J. Fuller.

25

Boxed, Elegant, and Imported 1822-1850

In 1822 Florida became a territory, William Bucknell blazed the Santa Fe Trail, steamers and flatboats plied the rivers, and packets and whalers sailed the sea. Wagons wheeled west over the growing National Road, and factories grew. James Monroe was president, and the population of the United States was 11,300,000. America was exuberant and nationalistic, and the fortunes of both the country and individuals were building. Commercial paper dolls came from Europe.

Paper dolls were imported from Europe. Tucked into the ships' holds were elegant paper dolls like Maria Taglioni.

In 1822 La Petite Psyche, an exquisite paper figure in a small gilt-edged box, was brought to America. Inscribed on the box was "This paper doll was brought from France by Mrs. Betty Welles in 1822 as a present for her daughter."

Immediately, one wonders about the little girl who received this treasure. She must have been transported with rapture. To receive such a gift she must also have been the child of America's growing wealthy, for elegant paper dolls such as these were toys for only a few.

La Petite Psyche is illustrated, and in the elegant, gold-embossed box came not only the charming small doll, but also a real, stand-up gilt mirror, six dresses, wraps, and hats. Its origin is listed as *Magazin du Mode.*

This is only one of the four Psyche dolls in the Waldron collection. There is another that was commercially lithographed in 1850 with a mirror inside the box; a child from the *Journal des Modes,* a delightful cutout in a handmade box with mirror and ribbon on the edges—1830-1839; and an 1835-1840 handmade French Psyche with mirror and stand, plus twenty-six dresses in Romantic, Taglioni style. The Museum of the City of New York also has in its collection the same La Petite Psyche that is illustrated.

It is clear that these charming dolls were made in some

La Petite Psyche. Imported from France in 1822.

numbers, and that those not fortunate enough to own a commercial doll made their own.

By 1830 the Erie Canal was operating; the first passenger train was laying track west; America had its first depression; Eli Whitney invented the cotton gin; and a frontiersman, Andrew Jackson, was president. He lent his name to an era that celebrated the rise of the common man. It was the period of Romanticism, of writers like Sir Walter Scott and Victor Hugo and composers like Chopin and Berlioz.

The first celebrity paper dolls come from the Romantic European ballet, and my discovery of one of these dolls in the summer of 1981 is an it-can-happen-to-you tale. There are still lots of treasures tucked away waiting to be discovered, and it is trite but true that they appear when least expected.

One morning I was invited to view a friend's paper doll. It had been rescued from beneath a pink ostrich fan in an otherwise empty dresser belonging to a recently deceased aunt. The furniture had been in storage for almost twenty years. The new owner believed the aunt to be the owner of the paper doll, and I expected to see an 1890s paper doll—a Tuck or *Herald* Lady.

The paper doll was Maria Taglioni, 1830s, in mint condition! My first glimpse of the doll was through a plastic baggy. The bright vivid embossed pink and gold-edged box caught the sun and gleamed through the plastic. It seemed to me, a paper doll fanatic, like a baggy of Bagdad jewels!

We put all the pieces of family information together and concluded that the Maria Taglioni doll must have come up the Ohio River on a flatboat to Louisville, Kentucky, with another family treasure, a full service of Limoges china, in the 1830s.

Maria Taglioni is illustrated. She was the premiere dancer of Paris. Hers was also the first celebrity paper doll. Thus, she reflects the popularity of the Romantic ballet in that period. She was born in 1804 and lived to be eighty. It was said she danced like a disembodied spirit, and, although dance *en pointe* began in the 1800s, Maria Taglioni perfected this technique.

Her father created her ballets. The first, *La Sylphide,* was for her debut in the Paris Opera in 1832, and with it, she inaugurated a new era in the history of the ballet. "Before Maria," writes Charles de Boigne, in *Petits Memoires de l'Opera,* "the dance was merely a profession, the profession of jumping as high as possible and pirouetting like a top . . . [in ballets] . . . based chiefly on Greek legends." In *La Sylphide,* Taglioni danced the role of a forest sprite who was loved by a Scottish lad. She thus popularized the Romantic fantasy in ballet.

Taglioni also made ballet fashion history in *La Sylphide.* Dance had been performed previously in classic tunic; in *La Sylphide,* Maria danced in a diaphanous belled skirt that was an immediate sensation and the prototype of the tutu. Thereafter, overskirts that were looped up on the left side, ornamented with a wreath of cut ribbons, and fastened with satin leaves and field flowers became a popular style—*a la Taglioni.* This lovely fashion can be seen in Maria's paper doll costumes. The Romantic themes of fantasy and the joys of the pastoral are also seen in Maria's costumes—from peasant to sprite.

The beautiful paper doll of Maria Taglioni incorporates many

of the characteristics common to the European boxed paper doll, the most elegant, expensive, and sought after of all paper dolls. Since numerous examples of these dolls will be shown in this book, I include all the characteristics here for future reference. All except the last two apply to Maria. (They also apply to ballerina Fanny Elssler, who follows.)

Characteristics of the European Paper Doll

- Beautiful, sturdy box with handsome decorative title in three languages—English, French, and German. (Sometimes Italian and Dutch are added.) These dolls are believed to have been printed for export trade.
- Gold edging on the box.
- Finely drawn dolls with close-cropped hair to facilitate headdressing.
- Costumes vividly colored and covered with shiny egg-white lacquer for protection.
- Sizes are varied. (Maria is known in three sizes: 4″, 5 3/8″, and 9 1/8″.)
- Front and back views of costumes.
- Front costume backed by plain green paper is believed to indicate German origin (characteristic of dolls from the 1850s).
- Two identical dolls appear in the set.

Fanny Elssler. Small paper doll of the ballerina of the Romantic period.
Courtesy of John Greene Chandler Memorial Museum, South Lancaster, Mass.

The Maria Taglioni paper doll was followed by one of Fanny Elssler, Viennese dancer of Paris, another Romantic ballerina. She was known for her fiery peasant dances, notably the *Spanish Cachucha,* the *Polish Cracovieene, La Gypsy,* and *La Tarentule.* The paper dolls illustrated are from the collection of Mr. Herbert Hosmer, and one can easily sense the verve and vitality for which Fanny was famous.

In 1840 Fanny Elssler toured America and was an unprecedented success. She was said to have returned to Europe with a fortune estimated at $500,000, a very large sum in 1840.

Opposite page: Maria Taglioni. Romantic ballerinas were the first celebrity paper dolls. C. 1835.
Courtesy of Museum of the City of New York

Fanny Elssler. Larger version of the Romantic ballerina, 9½″.
Courtesy of John Greene Chandler Memorial Museum, South Lancaster, Mass.

As you will note from the illustrations, the Fanny Elssler paper doll not only came in several sizes, but also the costumes of the large and small sets were different. This is unusual in European sets.

The ballerina Lucile Grahn, a Danish ballerina also popular in the Romantic ballet, was a paper doll, too. However, only her

Boxes, Fanny Elssler.
Courtesy of John Greene Chandler Memorial Museum, South Lancaster, Mass.

box lid has appeared to date, and it is in the collection of Mr. Hosmer. Perhaps, she, too, is waiting in an empty drawer for discovery.

Great progress occurred in American in the 1830s. Cyrus McCormick invented the reaping machine, and Goodyear discovered rubber vulcanization. In 1837 Queen Victoria was crowned Queen of England with pageantry and pomp. President Van Buren attended the event. Florence Hayward in *Century Magazine* (Vol. XXXII, 1897), looked back on the occasion in an article that said the woman was "tiny of stature, pathetically young, pathetically isolated, although so surrounded, this child-woman with her silvery voice, her grave yet sweet demeanor . . . [stood] . . . unmistakable in pose . . . [as] the Queen Victoria."

Queen Victoria at her coronation.
Lithograph from Century Magazine, *1897.*

Thus was crowned the queen who gave her name to the remaining years of 1800, thus happily simplifying terminology for all collectors and historians.

Paper lore (tales told by one collector to another) considers the illustrated paper doll from the late Mrs. Waldron's Winterthur collection to be Queen Victoria. The time frame is correct, and she is, of course, an imported doll, but she is minus an identifying box. However, she resembles the Queen. She is coiffured in Queen Victoria's style. She is richly bejeweled, and the Queen loved jewels. Her costumes are elegantly simple. However, the doll lacks the royal crown, robe, and scepter that would identify her definitively as Queen Victoria. Still, royal or not, this is a most beautiful, rare, and charming doll.

In the 1840s world and American progress in manufactured products accelerated. The United States was expanding. In 1841 the Oregon Trail opened up, and thousands of settlers headed for opportunities in the West. In 1845, as a result of the Irish potato famine, hundreds of thousands of Irish immigrants came to our shores to fill the growing factories and to serve in wealthy households. Samuel Morse invented the telegraph, and Elias Howe invented the sewing machine. There was talk of slavery and abolition. Paper dolls were still commercially elegant, boxed and imported, with the exception of those made by a little girl in Boston, who paid for her education by selling paper dolls. She is known as the girl from Munroe and Francis.

> They have been sold, for many years, at the book-store of Munroe & Francis, in Boston, where, I presume, they are still to be found. From different parts of New-England, and even from New York, little girls have sent to this store for a lady or a girl or a boy or a family, and have been delighted at receiving in exchange for their shilling, or quarter or half-dollar, an envelope, containing the doll and its pretty wardrobe, larger or smaller, with more or fewer dresses, according to its price.

This description is from the booklet *Paper Dolls and How to Make Them,* published in 1856 by Anson D. F. Randolph, 683 Broadway, New York City. No one knows the identity of this enterprising young lady, who put her handmade dolls into competition with boxed and imported dolls.

A beautiful series of imported European dolls from this time is also in the Winterthur collection of Mrs. Waldron. These are the American Lady and Her Children, the Lady of New York, and the Lady of London. These dolls are believed to have been designed for export, and incorporate the usual beautiful European characteristics. A boy and girl, plus wardrobes, are included with the American Lady.

Opposite page: Paper doll believed to be Queen Victoria. 1840.

Midcentury: The American Paper Doll

Even though the times were clouded by the issues of slavery and abolition, midcentury 1800 must have been an exciting time to be alive in America. Queen Victoria's consort, Prince Albert, staged the first spectacular world's manufacturers exhibit in the specially constructed iron and glass Crystal Palace in England, and America sent 650 exhibits with pride. Among them were rubber from Goodyear, false teeth, Colt's Repeating Pistol, McCormick's Reaper, chewing tobacco, and trotting sulkies.

In 1850, the average woman had seven children, and five lived. Clippers sailed from New York to Liverpool in twelve and one-half days, and in 1852 there was a direct rail line from New York to Chicago. The Gadsden Purchase added the territories of Nebraska and Kansas to the country. The Soo Canal was completed; the Suez began. Henry Bessemer invented the converter, and Darwin published his *Theory of Evolution*. In the year 1854 alone, 400,000 immigrants arrived in New York.

Chandler Memorial Museum

Most important to this book and the paper doll collector, commercial paper doll manufacture began in America. The first known commercial original paper doll is Fanny Gray. (*Little Fanny* and *Little Henry* toy books by J. Belcher of Boston in 1812 were copies of the English toy books.)

Fanny Gray is a story doll in the manner of the English toy books, complete with a tale and a head to slip into the back of a series of action costumes. The doll is exquisitely hand-drawn and watercolored, her box is hand-lettered, hand-constructed, and edged with gold, as illustrated. The title page is most elegantly decorated with delicate flower-strewn letters that read "Fanny Gray—May—1853." It is further illustrated with a lovely cottage scene. The story of Fanny Gray is handwritten in perfect penmanship on loose pages in the box.

There are three known complete copies of the handmade

Box and introduction to first lithographed American paper doll, Fanny Gray. Cosby, Nichols, and Company, 1854.

Courtesy of John Greene Chandler Memorial Museum, South Lancaster, Mass.

Fanny Gray and her costumes. Lithograph. Cosby, Nichols, and Company.

Beautiful box of handmade Fanny Gray. 1853.

Courtesy of John Greene Chandler Memorial Museum, South Lancaster, Mass.

Fanny Gray, and two are in the collection of Herbert Hosmer, great-nephew of John Greene Chandler. They are in the Chandler Memorial Museum, South Lancaster, Massachusetts.

Obviously, the handmade Fannys are the prototypes for the rare lithographed boxed toy book doll, *Fanny Gray,* published one year later by Cosby, Nichols, and Company, 111 Washington Street, Boston, Massachusetts, and lithographed by John Greene Chandler in 1854. This doll is considered to be the first original commercial American paper doll. (There *is* an English *Fanny Gray,* published by Dean and Sons of London. It is of later date, as established by Marion Howard in her book, *Those Fascinating Paper Dolls,* in which she makes a case for piracy from American to English—another first for *Franny Gray.*)

The artist-author of *Fanny Gray* is unknown. Mr. Hosmer believes it more than likely that the exquisite original dolls were executed by Sarah Peters, a professional miniature painter who married Leopold Grosslief, Chandler's chief European lithographer. He joined Chandler at that time. There is, however, another theory. The artist may have been Dorcas Smith, as the third original set is inscribed "Made for Gramma Dahl by her teacher, Dorcas Smith." "Perhaps," as Mr. Hosmer jokingly suggested, "the artist was the girl from Munroe and Francis." Perhaps.

No one knows the answers to this or other intriguing mysteries and gaps in paper doll information, and until definitive information appears, collectors conjecture. To most of us, conjecture is part of the fascination of the paper doll. There is still so much to discover, and it is, to a collector, as exciting as a Marco Polo trek to find one new snippet sifted from the past that fits into the paper doll puzzle and answers a question.

Fanny Gray is fact, not conjecture, and she makes an admirable first American paper doll. As with the English toy books, there is a story. In the lithographed set she is introduced:

> This little representation of Frances Gray . . . with the accompanying story . . . is intended as an amusement for children . . . and will, it is hoped be an acceptable present for the holidays. . . . The publishers have spared no expense . . . being desirous to present a beautiful specimen of the art of printing in color. The story begins:

> > Far from the noisy village street
> > Where the small brook's tinkly sound
> > Was heard the listening ear to greet
> > A little cottage once was found.

> > A stately oak-tree threw its shade
> > Just where the well-kept garden smiled
> > And there, from spring to autumn played
> > A happy, loving gentle child.

> > Widowed mother toiled within. . . .
> > And strove the daily bread to win. . . .
> > For pretty, gladsome Fanny Gray. . . .
> > She died and left her orphaned child to seek
> > Shelter in the world so wide. . . .

The plot of *Fanny Gray* chronicles Fanny's adventures from selling matches to helping Farmer Weston care for his chickens and sell their eggs, to caring for the sick farmer by selling flowers, to the happy ending—the recognition of flower-seller Fanny by a long-lost wealthy uncle who takes her in to live

> > With every longing gratified
> > With friends around her sunny way. . . .
> > Lives lovely petted Fanny Gray.

The dolls illustrated here are all from the collection of Mr. Hosmer, who has generously allowed so many of his paper dolls to be photographed for this book. Mr. Hosmer, I believe, is himself the "great enchanter of paper dolls" for he has established in the quiet, shaded, centuries-old town of South Lancaster, Massachusetts, a most magical, timeless, charming museum, the Toy Cupboard or John Greene Chandler Memorial Museum.

Open by appointment, this is the only paper doll and toy museum anywhere in the United States, and here, with unspoiled noncommercial charm, Mr. Hosmer not only displays Chandler paper dolls, children's books, paper toys, and doll's houses, but also produces puppet shows for birthdays and weekend entertainments, highlighted at holidays in the museum's grassy court by the crowning of local children as Queen of the Witches, Queen of Hearts, and Queen of the May. The May Queen's

THE JOHN GREENE CHANDLER MEMORIAL
(LITTLE BOOK HOUSE MUSEUM)
57 East George Hill Road
South Lancaster, Massachusetts 01561
(Founded 1951)

John Greene Chandler Memorial Museum commemorates John Greene Chandler, lithographer of Fanny Gray, America's first original paper doll.

scepter is a blue iris and her courtiers dance before her around the Maypole. (See Appendix for the museum's address.)

The museum's collection includes a complete display of lithographed Chandler paper dolls, which were published by Brown, Taggard, and Chase of Boston three years after Fanny Gray.

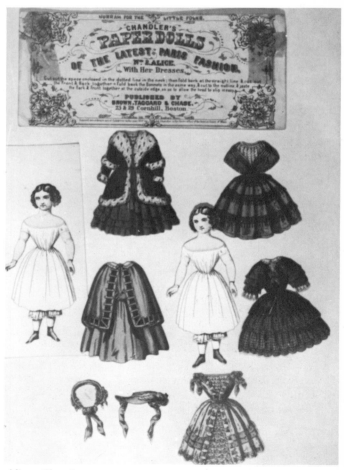

Alice. Chandler.
Courtesy of John Greene Chandler Memorial Museum, South Lancaster, Mass.

Charley. Chandler.
Courtesy of John Greene Chandler Memorial Museum, South Lancaster, Mass.

Little Fairy Lightfoot. Chandler.
Courtesy of John Greene Chandler Memorial Museum, South Lancaster, Mass.

These are full-figured paper dolls, beautifully detailed and delicately colored. They were sold in fancy envelopes labeled Hurrah for the Little Folks, which also advertised Chandler Paper Dolls of the Latest Paris Fashions. From 1857 they were published as follows:

No. 1 Carry
No. 2 Alice (illustrated)
No. 3 Charley (illustrated)
No. 4 Little Fairy Lightfoot (illustrated)
No. 5 Betty the Milkmaid
No. 6 Jack and His Pony

Besides the paper dolls, Mr. Chandler lithographed many paper toys and books. Probably the most well known is an original, the enduring classic *Chicken Little* (1840).

Dubois

I am indebted to Mr. Hosmer for the information that when John Greene Chandler's eyesight failed, Mr. Dubois became the designer and engraver for Brown, Taggard, and Chase of 25 and 29 Cornhill Road, Boston, Massachusetts. Dubois is responsible for the beautiful May Queen (illustrated) and Shepherdess. You will note that the envelope now reads Dubois rather than Chandler. Missing from the May Queen's accessories is a large May horn, which Mr. Hosmer states has turned up in one other collection.

Mr. Dubois is also credited with being the designer and engraver for Cousin Charles and Henry (illustrated), published by Cosby, Nichols, and Company, 117 Washington Street, Boston, in 1857. Envelope instructions that detail the cutting in such a way that the legs will fit into a stirrup suggest that a horse might have been originally included with the set.

The beautiful May Queen. Dubois.
Courtesy of John Greene Chandler Memorial Museum, South Lancaster, Mass.

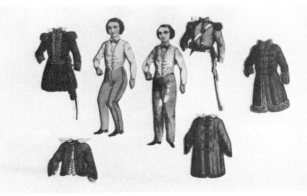

Cousin Charles and Henry. Dubois.
Courtesy of John Greene Chandler Memorial Museum, South Lancaster, Mass.

McCutchen Meadows, former home of Kentucky Library's Coke Collection, in the 1880s photo.
Photographed at Kentucky Library, Western Kentucky University.

Kentucky Library
Western Kentucky University

Researching a book can lead to great adventures for an author, and the finds at the Kentucky Library, Western Kentucky University, Bowling Green, Kentucky, were one of this book's greatest thrills.

My Delaware friend, Marilyn Forney, had seen a handmade paper doll display during a visit to the Kentucky Library Museum, so I contacted them. Finding a paper doll display at all is a thrill, because, due to space concerns, paper dolls are most often kept in storage and archives. Librarian Nancy Baird was responsible for this delight. In much enthusiastic, wonderful, and kind correspondence, she sent photocopies of the paper dolls in the Coke Paper Doll Collection, which had not been cataloged or sorted.

The dolls were exactly as they had emerged from the attic of a manor house called McCutchen Meadows, a land grant farm of 620 acres occupied for 150 years by the same distinguished family of McCutchens, Guthries, Cokes, and Underwoods. The ancestry of this family included James Guthrie, Secretary of the Treasury under President James Buchanan, and James Guthrie Coke, a signer of the revised Constitution of the Commonwealth of Kentucky. When the house was sold in 1980, the last of the family's owners William G. Coke donated many family papers to the Kentucky Museum for preservation. Among these were the paper dolls.

The Coke paper dolls were, to me, a magnificent archeological dig in two strata; a representatively complete 1850s stratum of American paper dolls as a child of the period played with them, and a second 1880–1890 stratum of beautifully executed handmade dolls. (See chapter on the Gilded Age.)

The dolls from the 1850s are described in the following pages. They include the first published American paper dolls like Chandler's Charley, Dubois's Cousin Henry, Austin, Clark, and Smith's Ella, Cinderella, and Nellie (illustrated), costumes of Hattie, envelope of Lillie Beers, McLoughlin's Susan Lee, dolls from the 1859 *Godey's Lady's Book,* Godey's fashion plates cut out, some made into dolls with handmade clothes, and two handmade dolls from 1850. Most excitingly, the collection contained the complete Anson Randolph paper family with six envelopes, which is, to my knowledge, the only complete family anywhere! You can imagine my collector's excitement and how much fun it was to sort and photograph these dolls for this book. I am most grateful to Nancy Baird and the Kentucky Library for this privilege.

It is also interesting, I think, to conjecture how the first American paper dolls were distributed through this representational group. They were published in Massachusetts and New York and completed in Kentucky.

Riley B. Handy, head of the Kentucky Library, believes the paper dolls originally belonged to the Underwood family, who then lived in Louisville. Were the dolls sold in a shop there? Louisville was a prosperous city. Mr. Hosmer has in his collection a large sign reading Chandler Dolls Sold Here, which presumably was either sold to or given to the retailers handling Chandler paper dolls. Perhaps paper dolls were part of a peddler's pack? We can only conjecture.

It is also intriguing that all these dolls preceded the Civil War (1859) in an area disrupted by war after 1861. There are no dolls of the late 1860s in this grouping. (The handmade dolls belong to a different generation of children.) One wishes these dolls could tell their tale.

Clark, Austin, and Smith

Obviously, the hour of paper doll publication had arrived in America, for the same year that Chandler published his series of paper dolls (Brown, Taggard, and Chase) and Dubois his (Cosby, Nichols, and Company), Clark, Austin, and Smith of New York brought out a series of paper dolls in envelopes called The Girls Delight.

Illustrated here are three sets of dolls found in the Coke Collection. Ten sets are believed to have been put out by Clark, Austin, and Smith in 1857. These are:

No. 1 Miss Florence
No. 2 Miss Hattie
No. 3 Master Frank
No. 4 Nellie (illustrated)
No. 5 Clara
No. 6 Cinderella (illustrated)
No. 7 The Little Pet
No. 8 Ella (illustrated, color section)
No. 9 Lillie Beers
No. 10 Emmie and Willie

The early New York paper dolls publishers were obviously well acquainted. The paper dolls of Clark, Austin, and Smith turn up as paper dolls of McLoughlin (the plates were probably sold to them by Clark, Austin, and Smith). The envelope of Miss Hattie, No. 2 in the Girls Delight series (part of which is in the Kentucky Library collection), gives the following instructions:

> All who have had number 1 (Florence) will understand how to prepare Hattie, her dresses & etc. Those who have not will learn all about it from a beautiful little book called "Paper Dolls & How to Make Them" . . . then Miss Hattie will look well enough to go to her sister's wedding.

Nellie. Clark, Austin, and Smith.
Photographed at Kentucky Library, Western Kentucky University.

As illustrated, the Clark, Austin, and Smith envelopes were each different and contained interesting messages for the child. Cinderella's tale shows that the moralistic story-toy was still popular in midcentury. It reads:

> From being a poor abused girl she came to great honor, you know, because she was so good and amiable. She treated her proud and haughty sisters kindly although they abused her.
>
> It is always true in real life as represented in the story that those who are good and kind and seek to make others happy, will be honored and happy themselves.

Cinderella. Clark, Austin, and Smith.
Photographed at Kentucky Library, Western Kentucky University.

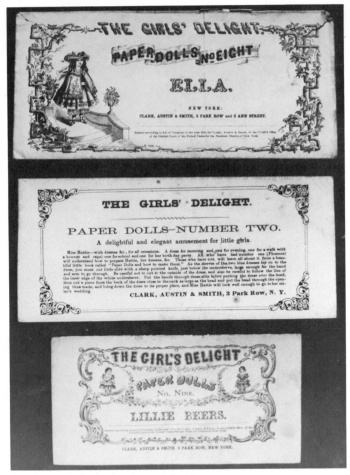

Envelopes of Clark, Austin, and Smith.
Photographed at Kentucky Library, Western Kentucky University.

Anson Randolph

In 1856 the firm of Anson Randolph published the little illustrated book *Paper Dolls and How to Make Them.* This charming book gives some early paper doll history and directions for making paper dolls. (See chapter on handmade dolls.) This book has been reproduced, and if an original can't be obtained, the reproduction is an excellent addition to the paper doll library.

This book was so popular that a second volume, *Paper Doll's Furniture, How To Make It,* was published in 1857. It was written by C. B. Allair. In the same year the *Paper Doll Family* was also published.

From *Those Fascinating Paper Dolls,* by Marion Howard, comes this advertisement:

> Who ever is enriched by the possession of "Paper Dolls" will wish to add the "Family" to their treasures. There are seven dolls, suitably colored, father, mother, sister, brother, and Bridget. These are furnished with a full colored wardrobe, ready to be cut out for use. FARMER . . . On receipt of seventeen Stamps, a copy of the Set in a wrapper, will be sent by mail, pre-paid.

Perhaps the Kentucky Anson Randolph family was ordered by mail.

The family is illustrated. There is large discrepancy in the artistic skill of the costumes for each doll. Howard makes note of this in *Those Fascinating Paper Dolls.* She states that Miss Adelaide has "four costumes, all original except the jacket dress at right of the envelope in the photographic illustration: this is a homemade dress."

The Kentucky Library Anson Randolph family's Miss Adelaide also had the handmade-looking "jacket dress," and without a comparison, I too would have reached Howard's conclusion—that the dress was homemade. However, incongruity of artistry is common to all the family costumes. Some seem skillfully printed, whereas others seem crudely done. The father, in particular, seems to have much handmade clothing.

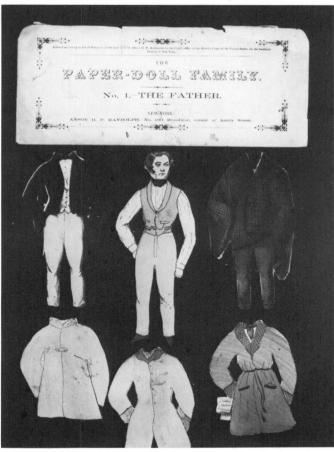

Father, Anson Randolph family. 8⁶/₈".
Photographed at Kentucky Library, Western Kentucky University.

Mother, Anson Randolph family. 5¹/₄".
Photographed at Kentucky Library, Western Kentucky University.

Miss Adelaide, Anson Randolph family. 4³/₄" (missing feet).
Photographed at Kentucky Library, Western Kentucky University.

It makes sense that, because American paper doll publication was in its infancy and the Anson Randolph author of *Paper Dolls and How to Make Them* demonstrated a somewhat primitive artistic skill, this firm probably used a combination of artists for the set without regard for the over-all appearance of the family. The coloring is very flat, indicating a stencil applied by hand with simply done woodcuts. *Harpers Weekly,* July 17, 1858, carries an Anson D. F. Randolph advertisement for "Leaf and Flower Pictures and How to Make. With 8 Colored illustrations $1.25. Containing full directions for the beautiful Art," indicating that the company produced items other than paper dolls.

Much more skillfully executed is National Costumes: A New and Instructive Amusement For The Young (illustrated), the

Clara, Anson Randolph family, 3³/₄".
Photographed at Kentucky Library, Western Kentucky University.

Bridget, Anson Randolph family, 5¹/₂".
(This was period of large Irish immigration.)
Photographed at Kentucky Library, Western Kentucky University.

Little Brother, Anson Randolph family. (A process of elimination makes this the little brother, dressed in girl-type clothing, common to fashion style of period.) 2³/₄".
Photographed at Kentucky Library, Western Kentucky University.

Baby. Anson Randolph family, 2¹/₂".
Photographed at Kentucky Library, Western Kentucky University.

Mother shows manner in which costumes must have been packaged. Each doll back has misaligned drawing on back and is half-size.

Photographed at Kentucky Library, Western Kentucky University.

only other paper doll known from this company. This is a beautiful and professional set. It was published in 1857 and has a box containing a booklet entitled *An Elegant and Instructive Amusement: With a Description of the Countries Where these Dresses Are Worn.* The booklet contains entertaining accounts of the countries illustrated. One follows:

> Hungary is now subject to the Emperor of Austria, but the Hungarians love their country and hope that it will again be free. There are high mountains in the North and East which keep off the cold winds, and make the climate mild. There are extensive forests in which are fierce wolves. The Hungarian nobles are very rich, and oppress the poor who live upon their lands.

McLoughlin Brothers

McLoughlin Brothers became the largest mass producers of paper dolls, and because of this, McLoughlin paper dolls are easy to find. The company was founded in 1828 by John McLoughlin, a Scottish coachmaker and carpenter. He arrived in this country in 1819 and worked for *The New York Times.* He went into business printing children's morality tracts on a second-hand press. In 1840 he merged with competitor John Elton, and they continued business under the Elton name. John McLoughlin, Jr., entered the business with his father, and when both his father and Elton retired, John changed the name of the company to McLoughlin Brothers. This firm became the first and largest producer of American children's books; it continued until 1920 when it was sold to Milton Bradley.

National costumes, Anson Randolph family.

Courtesy Henry Francis du Pont Winterthur Museum, Joseph Downs Manuscript Collection/
the Maxine Waldron Collection of Children's and Paper Toys

There are no copyright dates on McLoughlin paper dolls, but data has been carefully assembled by dedicated collectors. In *Those Fascinating Paper Dolls* (a must for McLoughlin collectors), Marion Howard presents a comprehensive chronological listing of McLoughlin addresses, garnered from the New York City Directory and researched by Bart Anderson of the Chester County Historical Society. Comparing these addresses with those on McLoughlin envelopes enables us to date the dolls they produced.

At their 24 Beekman Street address from 1854 to 1863, McLoughlin products were Frank, Jenny, and Lucy (first size); Baby, Dolly, Lizzie, Charley, Fanny, Little Lady, and Willie and His Pony (second size); and Bride, Grace Lee, Susan Lee, American Lady, Emma and Etty, and Adelaide (third size).

McLoughlin paper dolls were always presented in series and sizes according to price. The dolls were sold for many years, printed, reprinted, and added to. The first series included Lizzie (illustrated) and Susan Lee (illustrated, color section).

In 1978, Justin G. Schiller, Ltd., Antiquarian Book Seller,

Lizzie. Early McLoughlin doll, printed at 24 Beekman Street, New York City. (Because McLoughlin dolls were printed in great numbers, they are findable today.) **$35.**

Courtesy of Children's Museum of Indianapolis. Dolls not currently on exhibit.

offered for sale numerous original woodblocks from the archives of McLoughlin Brothers, purchased from Milton Bradley. The catalog issued for this sale clearly explains the early printing methods used by McLoughlin Brothers. According to the catalog, the artist cut the dolls from wood in the manner of the well known Naturalistic illustrator Thomas Bewick, who created a relief design on imported French boxwood in the same way metal is engraved. The engraver finished the job by turning the design into a printing block.

Many McLoughlin paper dolls bear the notation "stereotyped by Vincent Dill, 24 Beekman St., N.Y." This appears on the illustrated Susan Lee (color section). This practice, as defined and explained in Schiller's catalog, was a method used to preserve the original woodblocks from wear. Many engravers covered the original blocks with wax, made an impression from this, and cast the wax into metal. They printed with the latter, thus preserving the original blocks. The early McLoughlin printing method

consisted of printing the engraving over a colored tint block and applying detailed color by hand.

A comparison of the series produced at the first address with those done in the years 1864–1870 at the second, 30 Beekman Street, makes clear that the McLoughlin Brothers had greatly expanded, at the same time that, for one reason or another (age,

McLoughlin envelopes—listed series.
Courtesy of Children's Museum of Indianapolis. Dolls not currently on exhibit.

economics, or Civil War), other early paper doll publishers ceased publication. The phenomenal and enduring success of McLoughlin Brothers must have been due in part to the firm's great ability to keep pace with popular taste.

From the envelope illustrated, which lists McLoughlin paper dolls from 1864 to 1870, the popular is evident. Clara West was popular. Harriet Beecher Stowe's *Uncle Tom's Cabin,* abolitionist best-seller turned paper doll, and Eva St. Clair and Topsey selling for ten cents, were popular. Most popular of all the paper dolls were those from the New York American Museum: Tom Thumb, Minnie Warren, Commodore Nutt, and Mrs. Tom Thumb (illustrated, color section).

P. T. Barnum, called the Prince of Humbug in an era that adored humbug, discovered Tom Thumb by chance as the midget played games on the streets of Bridgeport, Connecticut. The child, Charles S. Stratton, was five years old and twenty-five inches tall. Barnum offered him three dollars a week to star in

Clara West. Early McLoughlin doll, 5⅝". **$60.** Chicago Historical Society photograph by Walter W. Krutz.

his American Museum. Of course, showman Barnum shuffled the child's biographical facts and ballyhooed Charles as General Tom Thumb, eleven years old and "just arrived from England."

Tom Thumb was an immediate success. The public loved him. He toured Europe, met royalty, and became wealthy. He was a capable businessman and invested well. He owned ponies, a yacht, and a house in Bridgeport that was built "Thumb" sized. In fact, Tom Thumb became so financially secure and happily occupied with his diversions, that Barnum had to find another small man to replace him at the museum.

His replacement was George Washington Morrison Nutt, a twenty-nine inch nineteen-year-old. Barnum named him Commodore Nutt. When Barnum discovered the twenty-four inch Lavinia Warren Bumpus from Middleboro, Massachusetts, trouping with a show, he added her to the museum.

Commodore Nutt was immediately smitten and proceeded to woo Lavinia while Tom Thumb was off playing with his ponies and yacht. Dropping in one day, Tom met Lavinia. He, too, was immediately smitten, and a great rivalry between the General and the Commodore began. Tom won.

Sarah Brown. McLoughlin 10¢ paper doll of the same series as Rosa Rustica. (City child, no doubt.) **$35.**
Courtesy of Children's Museum of Indianapolis. Dolls not currently on exhibit.

The wedding took place in Grace Church, New York, February 10, 1863. Two thousand guests were invited, and they included governors, congressmen, army and navy officers, and people from high society. President Lincoln sent his regrets and a set of Chinese firescreens. Commodore Nutt was best man, and Minnie Warren, the bride's small sister, was maid of honor. They were all immortalized in paper dolls by McLoughlin.

The couple honeymooned, toured Europe and the Orient, and had one child (also a paper doll). It lived, sadly, only two years. Tom died in 1883. Lavinia married an Italian midget and ran a country store in Massachusetts until her death in 1919.

Sometime in this period, McLoughlin Brothers acquired the paper doll plates of Clark, Austin, and Smith, and collectors will note on the illustrated envelopes the addition of names by Clark, Austin, and Smith to those sold by McLoughlin; i.e., Hattie, Ella (Ella Hall), Lillie Beers, Little Pet, Clara, Cinderella, and Nellie. Dolls from this period are illustrated.

Susie's pets. McLoughlin. Doll sold for 15¢, 6½". **$60.**
Courtesy of Children's Museum of Indianapolis. Dolls not currently on exhibit.

Godey's Lady's Book

Paper dolls were so popular in midcentury that *Godey's Lady's Book* published some considered to be the first magazine dolls in November, 1859. These dolls are illustrated. They consisted of a page of children printed in black and white, followed by a colored page of fashionable costumes. The whole was titled "For Little Girls Who Read Godey."

The color was hand-applied by "colorists," and the results were not always consistent and uniform. *Godey's* is said to have had occasional complaints from the readers that the blue morning gown in Boston was pink in Philadelphia. The same inconsistencies are noticed in different sets of the same hand-colored paper doll (McLoughlin; Austin, Clark and Smith; Chandler; and Anson Randolph). Of course, for collectors inconsistency adds to charm.

Oddly, it seems to collectors, the November issue of *Godey's* contained the only true paper doll they ever published, although fashion plates cut out were often termed "Godey's" paper dolls

Rosa Rustica. A remarkable McLoughlin doll. Probably one of the earliest paper dolls to illustrate the average child. (Most of the county was rural in this period.) **$35.**
Courtesy of Children's Museum of Indianapolis. Dolls not currently on exhibit.

by children. In 1977 Dover Publications issued a delightful and beautiful *Fashion Paper Dolls from ''Godey's Lady's Book'': 1840–1854,* and this lovely book is a must for contemporary collectors.

Godey's Lady's Book *doll. First magazine paper doll, 1859.* $35 (both). Addison Collection

Godey's Lady's Book *doll. Colored page.* Addison Collection

Mysteries

From the collection of the Essex Institute, Salem, Massachusetts, comes the paper doll Gertrude (illustrated). She illustrates the story of the same name written by Maria Susanna Cummins in 1854. This doll was published in Hartford by E. B. and E. C. Kellog. Gertrude is another toy book with a separate head. Her six costumes tell a well known tale, ''The Lamplighter,'' which has been retold in several books. It is not known if this doll accompanied the original publication of the story, but it is obviously from this general time period.

From the Cooper-Hewitt Museum in New York City come

Gertrude, the heroine of ''The Lamplighter.'' E. B. Kellog. Story doll by Susanna Cummins that became ''The Lamplighter.'' Courtesy of The Essex Institute, Salem, MA

Gertrude, the heroine of
"The Lamplighter."
Courtesy of The Essex Institute, Salem, MA

American paper dolls of the
Cooper-Hewitt Museum.

Cooper-Hewitt Museum,
The Smithsonian Institution's
National Museum of Design

the lovely ladies illustrated. They are listed as American paper dolls. Their publisher is not known, and they await further identification.

Kimmel and Foster, well-known lithographers of midcentury, are known to have published one beautiful boxed paper doll, The American Lady and Her Children (illustrated). The Winterthur Museum has amongst its paper dolls a beautiful lithographed, boxed Realm of the King of Flowers fancifully done by this company, and collectors hope more paper dolls by this publisher will come to light in time.

American paper dolls of the Cooper-Hewitt Museum.

Cooper-Hewitt Museum, The Smithsonian Institution's National Museum of Design

The American Lady and Her Children. Kimmel and Foster.   Courtesy of Museum of the City of New York

45

Jenny Lind, with costumes from operatic performances. Courtesy of Museum of the City of New York

Imported European doll. Courtesy of Children's Museum of Indianapolis. Dolls not currently on exhibit.

Imported 1850-1870

Because Americans of the Victorian era were impressed and influenced by the styles, fashion, and culture of Europe; because wealthy American children played with paper doll elegances imported from Europe; and because the rare European boxed dolls are most highly prized by today's collectors, the more notable imported paper dolls are illustrated here. These dolls retain the characteristics of imported paper dolls mentioned earlier in this book.

Jenny Lind, 1860–1869. In 1851 Jenny Lind, the Swedish Nightingale, toured America under the auspices of P. T. Barnum. Fanny Morris Smith, in *Century Magazine* (Vol. XXXII, 1897), recreated her visit thus:

> The public was mad about her. Wherever she sang, every window and roof for blocks from the concert hall was packed with people waiting to see her pass. . . . In America were repeated the scenes of London where the frantic rush of people fighting their way toward her had generated a new name—the Jenny Lind crush.

Jenny Lind was born in Stockholm in 1820. She first sang in London in 1847 and "all London went mad for her." She was remarkable both for her voice and for the naturalness and purity of her art. Her repertoire combined operatic arias with folk music.

Paper lore states that Jenny Lind herself suggested that children would enjoy her paper doll. The dolls were published in three sizes and costumed from her most famous roles, as illustrated.

Jenny Lind.

Bride Doll. Unidentified European set. Courtesy of Children's Museum of Indianapolis. Dolls not currently on exhibit.

Boy. Courtesy of Children's Museum of Indianapolis. Dolls not currently on exhibit.

Costumes for young man. Courtesy of Children's Museum of Indianapolis. Dolls not currently on exhibit

From the Indianapolis Children's Museum. From the Children's Museum in Indianapolis comes an exquisite set of paper dolls, including two lady figures, a girl, and a boy (all illustrated). These dolls are without an identifying box. They are identical to those drawn in *Paper Dolls: A Guide to Costume,* by Clara Hallard Fawcett, who called them John and Mary. They are, of course, imported from Europe.

Notice the similarity in the children's costumes and accessories with those shown in the following imported dolls. They all are indeed richly endowed, portraying activities and entertainments approved of in the period.

The Brave Boy, 1850–1859. From the magnificent Winterthur collection of the late Maxine Waldron comes The Brave Boy, The Virtuous Girl, A Boy and Girl, The Industrious Lady, and The Biggest and Most Beautiful Doll. These are splendid paper dolls. They are small masterpieces and more fit, it seems to me, for a nook in the Louvre than for a noisy Victorian nursery.

Indeed it is probable that such fine paper dolls as these were reserved for careful, quiet play in the best parlor by ladylike children. Of course, encouraging care, maternal instincts, and housewifery with exceptionally beautiful and well-made toys was a Victorian precept of childrearing. Judging from the complete sets of handsome dolls remaining from the period, the instruction must have been successful.

The Brave Boy's costumes are symbolic and represent Victorian attributes toward bravery. As you will note in the illustration, with a sword the young man is brave, with his globe he is studious, as a hunter he is assiduous or diligent, with flowers he is sincere, and with bags of money for the beggars he is liberal or generous.

The Virtuous Girl, 1860–1869. The beautiful boxed paper doll (illustrated), contains "eight representations to be changed." Once again, the costumes are symbolic. This time they represent feminine Victorian virtues: candor (with doves), patience (with the baby), clemency (cleaning pot), beauty (with dog), application (with the hoe), gentleness (with the lamb). Missing from this set are costumes for diligence and sincerity. This set is found complete in the toy museum in Nurnberg, Germany.

Boy and Girl, 1850–1859. This charming "togetherness" pair of dolls also comes in action-posed representations. Pantomimes and charades were popular pastimes in the Victorian era, and these dolls posed in motion seem lovely tableaux of approved youthful occupations.

As there is no definitive box to explain the symbolism of this pair, if it exists, the collector must use his imagination. The Victorian sentimental, idealized relationships of male to female are quaintly evident here. In each little scene the male is most protective of the female.

The Industrious Lady, 1850–1859. If one were to write a history of women illustrated by the paper doll, The Industrious Lady would be a good beginning choice. This doll is a beautiful example of perfect, prosperous, graceful Victorian womanhood. She is a lovely lady who spends her time as the period admonished from pulpit to periodical: "not in idleness but in improving tasks."

Girl.
Courtesy of Children's Museum of Indianapolis. Dolls not currently on exhibit

Brave Boy.
Courtesy Henry Francis du Pont Winterthur Museum, Joseph Downs Manuscript Collection/
The Maxine Waldron Collection of Children's and Paper Toys

Boy and Girl. Courtesy Henry Francis du Pont Winterthur Museum, Joseph Downs Manuscript Collection/The Maxine Waldron Collection of Children's and Paper Toys

She is presented in a series of representations, in this case "genre" settings. In fascinating detail and vivid, rich color, the lady spins, sews, embroiders, makes hats, lace, and flowers. She draws and paints. She is always costumed suitably for the time of day and her occupation.

Plain green backing completes her costumes, indicating German origin. She is liberally shiny with egg-white, and her box is marked FRK.

The Greatest and Most Beautiful Doll, 1849–1850. Christened Sophy and Lilly by their owners, these large and beautiful paper dolls would be of special interest to researchers of the toy.

The dolls are finely drawn, and because of their large size, their toys are clearly defined. The collector will note that the doll's doll has a face that resembles its owner's. Two ball games, unfamiliar to me, are depicted with the dolls. One costumed doll holds a heartshaped racket and a small, hard ball. Another costumed doll holds a ball on a string with a pendant at the end. Perhaps the reader can identify these activities.

The box of this doll, titled in four languages, shows two little girls playing with the two identical dolls included. This would seem to indicate that the European purpose of the dual dolls was not merely insurance against doll loss, but also a practice to facilitate the sharing of dolls and costumes.

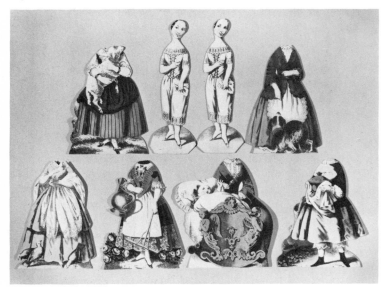

Virtuous Girl.
Courtesy Henry Francis du Pont Winterthur Museum,
Joseph Downs Manuscript Collection/
The Maxine Waldron Collection of Children's and Paper Toys.

The Greatest and Most Beautiful Doll. Courtesy Henry Francis du Pont Winterthur Museum, Joseph Downs Manuscript Collection/The Maxine Waldron Collection of Children's and Paper Toys

Handmade–Homemade

In 1856 an unknown female wrote the previously discussed *Paper Dolls and How To Make Them* for publisher Anson Randolph. This book was a great success and was followed by *Paper Doll's Furniture: How To Make It.*

Because the Randolph book inspired so many thousands of little girls to make paper dolls, I would like to share parts of it with you. In practical instructions the author directs the readers to use

> any kind of stiff paper, the backs of old card, paste-board, Bristol board . . . for the dresses, I dare say your father will give you the colored covers of old pamphlets. The unprinted backs of these are better than the glazed colored papers you find at bookstores because you can paint upon them. . . . There is scarcely any kind of paper, even brown wrapping paper, out of which you cannot make something pretty for your little ladies and gentlemen. Colored note paper or letter paper is perhaps most desirable material. The colored tissue ''motto-Papers'' make elegant party dresses. . . . If after your first doll is finished you should say ''What a horrid-looking thing'' . . . do not destroy it . . . give it to your little sister . . . she will be delighted and call it ''Pooty baby.''
>
> If you cannot succeed in making respectable-looking faces, you can perhaps find some fashion-plate at the end of an old magazine, a suitable head, which your mother will allow you to cut off and paste upon a body of your own making . . . for these fashionable things have no real bodies, their dress is the whole of them.

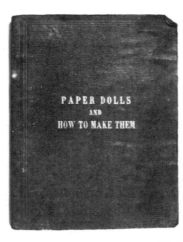

Paper Dolls
and How to Make Them.
Anson Randolph.

Illustration from Paper Dolls and How to Make Them. *Anson Randolph.*

Estrella Beauharness, Marion Leland, and George Fortune. All reside in bronchial troches box.

Favorite handmades of my collection are the tiny primitive Estrella Beauharness, her beau, George Fortune, and her best friend, Marion Leland (illustrated). Less than 2″ tall, this handmade trio came to me in a wonderful small Brown's Bronchial Troches box. These dolls date in the 1850s. Their enormous wardrobes are cut just as the Randolph book advises, from card and pamphlet, as evidenced by their backs. Tiny cross-stitch decorates the clothing; bits of store-bought glazed paper decorate the costumes. Many tiny dolls handmade in varying degrees of skill have been found from this period, and it must have been a child-fad of the period to do this delicate work.

Dancing Dolls. In the 1860s *Godey's* gave instructions for dancing dolls, articulated figures much like the pantin. They were to be fancifully dressed in tissues and laces, ribbons and flowers. They were a popular fad, and many lovely examples are to be found.

Scraps. Technically, scraps are sheets of cutout fancies like flowers, cherubs, birds, Santas, mottos, animals, and so on, printed beginning in the 1860s in Germany and France.

They were exported to this country to be used in the popular hobby of making scrapbooks. The greatest production of scraps was between 1875 and 1900, and the best known and largest producer was Raphael Tuck, English printers with works in Saxony, Germany. This firm was also known for its beautiful paper dolls, valentines, and Christmas cards.

From scrap to paper doll was a short step for a child, and quaint examples of their art exist in abundance. A particularly appealing waifish scrap doll is illustrated.

Over the years ''scraps'' has become a paper lore term for the childhood custom of cutting figures from catalogs and fashion magazines and playing with these as with paper dolls.

I have a friend with hundreds of figures cut from *Godey's* and *Peterson's* by an ancestor. Over the years they have been passed along as Grandma's dolls, and, if they have no great monetary collector's value, they have enormous sentimental appeal.

Dancing Doll.
Courtesy of Museum of the City of New York

Wistful Scrap Doll.
Courtesy of Children's Museum of Indianapolis. Dolls not currently on exhibit.

Paper lore calls these fashion figures cut from a magazine and played with as a paper doll, scraps. *Coke Collection.*
Photographed at Kentucky Library, Western Kentucky University.

Handmades of the Kentucky Library. The Kentucky Library includes in their Coke paper doll collection not only the wonderful early paper dolls of American publishers, but also numerous artistically made, exquisite handmade paper dolls. Unfortunately, there is space to show only a few. These wonderful dolls span twenty years, and all have notations such as ''the dolls Fanny made for me.'' In combination they present a bright vision of little girls from long ago in happy play. Once again, one wishes paper dolls could tell their tale.

Handmade doll from 1850s.
Coke Collection.

Photographed at Kentucky Library, Western Kentucky University.

Handmade Elegant Lady, 1890.
Coke Collection.

Photographed at Kentucky Library, Western Kentucky University.

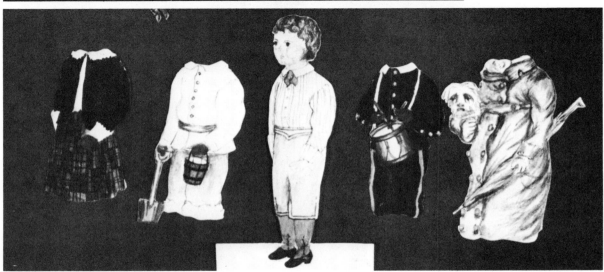

Handmade doll from Indianapolis.

Courtesy of Children's Museum of Indianapolis.
Dolls not currently on exhibit.

Made for Anita Blair. The Chicago Historical Society has a treasure in two handmade scrapbooks that were "Made for Anita Blair." The scrapbooks are illustrated. The silver book with acorns and stag head is the older of the two. It is inscribed: "Painted for Anita C. Blair—63 years ago by Baltimore Decorative Art Society. A gift from her mother and father, Mr. and Mrs. Henry A. Blair."

Cutting out furniture and pasting it into rooms to make paper dollhouses is, like scrap paper dolls, a traditional pastime handed down through the generations, along with hopscotch, hide and seek, cops and robbers, and playing house or dress up. It was, before television, plastic, and structured time changed childhood, an enchantment for rainy days, sick days, hot days, long days, days with best friends, or days spent alone.

The scrapbooks made for Anita Blair utilize this time-honored technique, cutting furnishings from catalogs and periodicals to make scrapbook houses for paper families, but these scrapbooks were made by talented adults and are works of art.

The earliest, the Baltimore book, dates in the 1890s. The second book came later and was painted by Miss Jenks, a student at the Chicago Art Institute. Both are in beautiful watercolor.

The first scrapbook has fifteen rooms done by the Society and three done by a child. A room, of course, is the book open and laid flat, with the rooms pasted on the two open pages. Doors to closets, cupboards, pantry, and so on, are cut to open, and a piece of paper is pasted behind to show what is behind the door.

The Baltimore book's rooms include entry hall, drawing room, study, dining room, music room, conservatory, three bedrooms, nursery with toys, bathroom, pantry, kitchen, and formal garden. The second scrapbook is as extensive as the first and includes an exterior view of the house, a game room, a study with a Turkish corner (a Victorian vogue, stylishly swish), and a door that opens to a view of "Ceylon Court, the original Ceylon Building from the first Chicago's World's Fair moved to Williams Bay, Wisconsin, by a friend of the Blairs."

Greek statues, cutout pictures (Mark Twain, Civil War officers, Gibson Girls, actresses), books, a gramophone, a mandolin, a packet of letters, scarves, aspidistras, an ice cream freezer, toys—the wondrous litter of life lavishly fills these rooms for the large paper family and their servants to enjoy.

These books, and others made by children, are treasures of the past and a legacy to the future. I hope they inspire imitation.

Anita Blair's Scrapbooks. Chicago Historical Society photograph by Walter W. Krutz.

54

Kitchen of scrap house made for Anita Blair. Chicago Historical Society photograph by Walter W. Krutz.

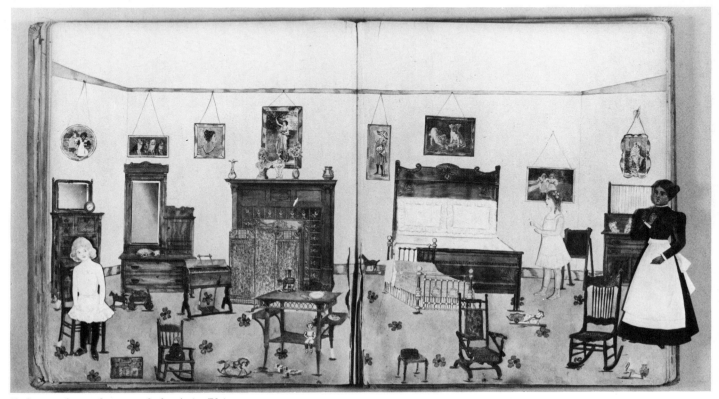

Bedroom of scrap house made for Anita Blair. Chicago Historical Society photograph by Walter W. Krutz.

Diane, The Bride. McLoughlin Brothers. Courtesy of Children's Museum of Indianapolis. Paper dolls not currently on exhibit.

Fanny Gray. Handpainted watercolor title.

Courtesy of John Greene Chandler Memorial Museum, South Lancaster, Mass.

Fanny Gray. Handpainted watercolor sets were the first original American paper dolls sold commercially.

Courtesy of John Greene Chandler Memorial Museum, South Lancaster, Mass.

Anson Randolph Family.

Photographed at Kentucky Library, Western Kentucky University.

Ella. Clark, Austin, and Smith.

Photographed at Kentucky Library, Western Kentucky University.

Tom Thumb and Mrs. Tom Thumb. McLoughlin Brothers. Chicago Historical Society photograph by Walter W. Krutz.

Susan Lee. McLoughlin Brothers. **$80.**

Baby Blue. McLoughlin Brothers. **$60.**

The Industrious Lady. Imported European paper doll, c. 1860–69.

Courtesy, Henry Francis du Pont Winterthur Museum, Joseph Downs Manuscript Collection/The Maxine Waldron Collection of Children's and Paper Toys.

The Boston Herald Lady. **Dolls $8 each. Costumes $3.50 each.** Chicago Historical Society photograph by Walter W. Krutz.
Left to right:
February 2, 1896; July 14, 1895; June 8, 1895; May 12, 1895; February 9, 1896; May 26, 1895; April 28, 1895; September 1, 1895; July 7, 1895.

The Boston Herald Lady. **Dolls $8 each. Costumes $3.50 each.** Chicago Historical Society photograph by Walter W. Krutz.
Left to right:
Doll; April 21, 1895; September 29, 1895; August 25, 1895; Doll; June 30, 1895; October 1895; June 9, 1895.

Scrapbook made for Anita Blair.   Chicago Historical Society photograph by Walter W. Krutz.

Cinderella. Raphael Tuck. **$40.** Addison Collection

Lettie Lane. Drawn by Sheila Young for Ladies' Home Journal. **$15.**

Fair Frances. Raphael Tuck. **$40.**

Dolly Dingle. Drawn by Grace Drayton for Pictorial Review. **$15.**

Addison Collection

Wedding of the Paper Dolls. Merrill. Drawn by Lucille Webster. $35.
Courtesy of Merrill Co., Publishers (Jean Woodcock)

Winnie Winkle. Gabriel. $40.
Courtesy Tribune Company Syndicate, Inc. Addison Collection

The Fashion Shop. Saalfield, 1938. $35.
Addison Collection. Courtesy Rand McNally & Co.

Winnie and Her Stylish Wardrobe.
Courtesy Tribune Company Syndicate, Inc. Addison Collection

Gone with the Wind. Pages of book, cover, and dolls. Merrill, 1940. **$150, up.**

The Gilded Age 1870–1900

"Godliness is in league with riches," Boston Bishop William Lawrence philosophically preached in the last years of the 1800s. Assuredly, most of his congregation nodded approval as they considered their own determined and vigorous pursuit of the popular American dream of wealth, respectability, and culture.

Less was not more in the Victorian era. More needed more, and more was produced. By 1900 there were 4,000 millionaires in the country. Income tax was unheard of, and great fortunes were amassed. Gould, Fiske, Vanderbilt, Carnegie, and Astor were magic names. Mrs. William Astor was queen of New York. Society was the Four Hundred who fit into her ballroom, summered at Newport or Saratoga, wintered in Florida, sojourned abroad, and reveled in everything sumptuous. Mark Twain christened this "The Gilded Age," and, as ever, paper dolls mirrored the popular.

McLoughlin Brothers

Increased industrialization produced not only great wealth, but also a large middle class whose tastes included and approved paper dolls. McLoughlin Brothers expanded, opening a new factory in Brooklyn in the 1870s, which, according to the Justin G. Schiller Ltd. catalog of original woodblocks from the archives of McLoughlin Brothers, was the "largest color printing plant in the country." Here McLoughlin published children's books, freely plagiarizing the English Kate Greenaway and Ralph Caldecott picture books that were unprotected by copyright. They also published many American favorites, such as *Rip Van Winkle* and *A Visit from St. Nicholas,* illustrated by Thomas Nast.

Paper doll production equaled that of picture books, and McLoughlin continued producing dolls in series, keeping the old favorites like the Tom Thumb crew from Barnum's American Museum and the Austin, Clark, and Smith dolls, and adding new

ones. There was a new series of fiteen-cent dolls with wonderful names: Dottie Dimple, Susie Simple, and Bertie Bright. There were new ten-cent dolls: Bessie Bliss, Lottie Love, and Myra Mild. New five-cent dolls were: Polly Prim, Gerty Good, and Jenny June. Some are illustrated.

McLoughlin envelope listing their series.
Courtesy of Children's Museum of Indianapolis. Dolls not currently on exhibit.

Daisy. McLoughlin. Cost 5¢. **$35.** Addison Collection

Florence. McLoughlin. Cost 1¢. **$25.**

Bessie Bliss. McLoughlin. Sold for 10¢. **$35.**
Courtesy of Children's Museum of Indianapolis. Dolls not currently on exhibit.

Envelope for Baby Blue. Chicago Historical Society, photograph by Walter W. Krutz.

Baby Blue. McLoughlin. 10⅝". Not a delicate, pastel infant, Baby Blue is flounced and ruffled in Dolly Varden, Victorian style. $65.

During this period, the gaudy Dolly Varden paper doll series was issued, named probably for the popular Dolly Varden fashion style of the 1870s, which called an overskirt of printed material pulled back with ruffles and bows to form a back bustle a Dolly Varden. All the dolls in the series wear this style, including my

66

favorite, the improbable Baby Blue, a giant baby whose costumes are bright red. The fashion name is said to be derived from Dolly Varden, a character in Charles Dicken's *Barnaby Rudge,* who dressed in the Watteau style. There are three dolls in the series: Baby Blue (illustrated), Bertha Blonde, and Betsy Brunette. Also issued was a less expensive Little Dolly Varden series of six dolls, including Clara Louise Kellog the opera singer and Charlie Varden, whose costumes include a Union Army uniform.

The effects of the Civil War were still felt in the country, and it is interesting to think of paper dolls in the light of the following letter to the editor from *Peterson's Magazine,* published in 1873:

New Employment for Women—Putting aside the vexed question of the new claims of women, one right they undoubtedly have, which nobody would deny them, that of life, and a means, if need be, of supporting it honestly. They must eat, and work for something to eat, if they have nobody to work for them. Since the war, the number of women thus forced, willingly or unwillingly, to earn their own way is largely on the increase. Their usual methods of bread-winning, teaching and sewing, are overcrowded and if some new paths had not been found for them, many would be driven to starvation. In the larger cities such new paths have been opened, and all right-feeling, sensible men and women are glad of any new way, both honorable and womanly, by which their struggling poorer sisters can help themselves and their children. Chief among these handicrafts are the numerous applications of any artistic talent which a woman may possess, to the services of arts or manufacturers. Women are now employed as colorists in photographic galleries, as engravers on wood, steel and stone, on almost any kind of industry where delicacy of eye and touch is required.

Most certainly, women, widows of the Civil War in particular, were employed by McLoughlin, the largest publisher of children's books and games, and they must have been employed in making paper dolls.

In the McLoughlin Catalog of 1887, when they were housed at 623 Broadway, the French series of paper dolls appeared. They came in two sizes, one in sheets and one "in envelopes in color and gold." These dolls were "elegantly printed in colors": Marie Louise and Henri; Antoinette and Irene; Diane, the Bride (illustrated); Virginie; Pauline, Baby and Anette; and Eugenie and Hortense.

The change in construction is interesting. Backs and fronts were now separate and were no longer attached to each other. Clothes now had tabs to hold them on the doll.

Diane, the Bride. McLoughlin. From the French Series of the 1880s. $65. Courtesy of Children's Museum of Indianapolis. Dolls not currently on exhibit.

Katie. 6¼″. Came in sheet to be cut out. **$15.**

Mamie. McLoughlin. **$15.**

Dennison's were wonderfully creative paper dolls. **$65.**

McLoughlin Brothers issued many dolls over the company's history, and they repeated favorites for decades. It would take a complete book to illustrate all their dolls, if all could be found. Marion Howard's *Those Fascinating Paper Dolls* does include all that have been found, and an antique paper doll collector should own this wonderful book, which is a current reissue by Dover Publications.

Adding to the old dolls in series, McLoughlin issued in the 1890s dear little girls like Katie (illustrated), Lizzie, Mamie (illustrated), and Nellie.

Peter G. Thompson Company

A smaller paper doll publisher of the 1880s was the Peter G. Thompson Company of Cincinnati, Ohio. This firm was responsible for a series of at least six dolls somewhat similar in appearance to those of McLoughlin. Unfortunately unavailable for illustration here, they included Pansy Blossom, Flora McFlimsy, and Jessie Jingle for fifteen cents; Daisy Deane, Lillie Lane, and Susie Bell for ten cents; and Bessie Bright, Nellie Bly, and Flora Frizzle for eight cents each.

Dennison Manufacturing Company

Sometime in the 1880s, Dennison Manufacturing Company added crepe paper to their tissue paper, delighting little girls and beginning a paper doll fashion that lasted for at least forty years and combined the creativity and fun of the handmade—homemade paper doll with the store-bought, commercial paper doll. Beautifully printed and imported from Germany, where they were made by Littauer and Bauer, these articulated dolls were sold separately and in boxes, with dolls and crepe papers and trims. The child created her own dresses. These dolls were so popular, that examples are numerous and are quite easily found by the collector. Some are illustrated.

Edith Flack Ackley, in *Paper Dolls, Their History and How To Make Them*, reminisces that . . .

> The first store-made paper dolls I can remember were about 7½ inches tall. They came with light and dark hair and their arms and legs were fastened on with little metal gadgets that made them moveable.
>
> My father bought them for me from Dennison's in New York probably around 1897. I remember also that I had never seen colored tissue paper before then, except pink. The papers were displayed most attractively on a special rack, and I had great fun picking out the different shades of colors. One special sheet of paper in pink and blue was a check design which I used most economically.

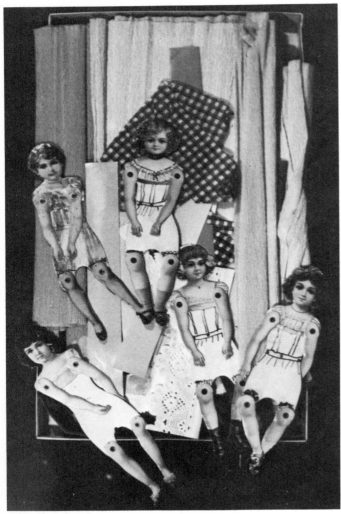

Dennison dolls wait to be dressed. **$65.**

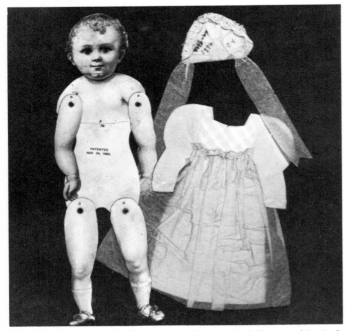

Dennison baby, beautifully dressed. Handmade dolls are subjectively priced. There are numerous specimens of this type of popular doll, and they make a most delightful addition to any collection.

Ruffled Dennison doll.
Dennison dolls courtesy of Children's Museum of Indianapolis. Dolls not currently on exhibit.

Frederick A. Stokes Company

The Federick A. Stokes Company Publishers issued several beautiful and highly collectible paper doll sets in New York in the 1890s. A Year Of Paper Dolls was published in 1894, Prince and Princesses in 1895, and Famous Queens and Martha Washington (illustrated) in 1895.

The Prince and Princesses and The Famous Queens and Martha Washington are lovely portrait paper dolls done by artist Elizabeth Tucker. Mary, Queen of Scots; Louis, Dauphin of France; Albert Edward, Prince of Wales; Crown Princess Wilhelmina of Holland; Crown Prince Wilhelm Frederick of Germany; Infanta Marguerite of Spain; a little American girl of 1895, titled an American Princess, were included in the charming Prince and Princesses set.

The Famous Queens and Martha Washington portray Queen Isabella of Spain, Queen Elizabeth of England, Queen Margherita of Italy, Queen Louise of Prussia, Queen Marie Antoinette of France, Queen Victoria of England, and our own Martha Washington.

Advertising Paper Dolls

In the late 1880s and early 1890s, advertising developed product merchandising. Paper dolls were popular, easy, and cheap to produce, easy to insert into packages, and easy to mail. The paper doll was a natural choice for advertising, and premium paper dolls were produced in this period in such large quantities that they are a collection specialty in themselves. They are comparatively easy to find.

The Famous Queens. F. A. Stokes. **$150.** Courtesy of Cynthia Musser.

Advertising dolls from 1890s. Bottom, left to right: Lion Coffee riding series Brownie **$8**; *Pillsbury Flour (Forbes doll)* **$6**; *Baker Chocolate English Soldier* **$2**; *Shaker Salt King, Queen, and Shaker Lady* **$10**; *Enameline Princeton College series* **$3**.

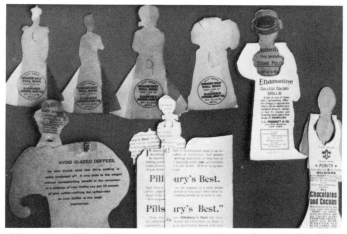

Advertising dolls. Their messages are displayed on back. Note Forbes's construction of Pillsbury Flour Lady.

These paper dolls, along with trading cards, sold almost every product. They were made in series to be collected, and all had the advertiser's message on their backs.

Enameline Stove Polish
Requires No Mixing
Produces a Jet, Black Enamel Gloss
Makes No Dust or Dirt
Will not Rust or Injure the Stove
ENAMELINE
Is Never Peddled

So says Rose, the Enameline paper doll. Pansy, Poppy, Chrysanthemum, Violet, and Primrose paper dolls, sisters to Rose, could be obtained by ''sending three two cent stamps to J. L. Prescott Co.''

Listed here are some of the best known and most highly sought series of advertising dolls.

Clarks O.N.T. Thread makers; wedding series (illustrated); minuet series.

Shaker Salt. Travels of the Shaker Salt Lady told in story (illustrated); paper dolls representing monarchs met on trip. Fifteen doll series.

Swifts. Calendar dolls, four large, 19" dolls, each holding three one-month calendars.

Lion Coffee. Palmer Cox Brownies; Riding Brownies series and Standing Brownie series (illustrated). Also occupational series.

Diamond Dye. Little girls with dye pot and dresses.

McLaughlin Coffee. Best-known queens. According to collector Edith White, there were over 1,000 different dolls produced in series.

None Such Mince Meat. Little girls in foreign costumes, made by Forbes Lithographing and woven together.

Pillsbury. Series of dolls with background showing flour (illustrated). Forbes weaving (illustrated).

Hood. Sarsaparilla family of five dolls with two costumes each.

Dover Publishing has issued *Antique Advertising Paper Dolls* (selected and edited by Barbara Whitton Jendrick), which is complete to the messages on the dolls' backs.

Singer Sewing Girl. **$10.** Addison Collection

70

Wedding Party. Assembled, O. N. T. **Set $50.** Courtesy of Edna Corbett

The *Boston Herald* Lady

The merchandising value of paper dolls was discovered in the 1890s, and newspapers added dolls to their news supplements in this period to help sell newspapers. The *Boston Herald* Lady, a collector's favorite, was printed each Sunday from 1895 to 1896 by the *Boston Herald* and other newspapers. The dolls illustrated here come from the *Chicago Record*. Two dolls were issued, and additional dolls could be sent for by mail. Costumes appeared weekly.

If I were to continue that history of women illustrated by the paper doll mentioned earlier, I would choose the *Boston Herald* Lady as the second in the Paper Doll Women's Progress Parade. Compared with the Industrious Lady of 1850, the *Herald* Lady shows the new active lives that women in trimmer skirts were enjoying. The *Herald* Lady rode horseback, played tennis, yachted, bathed, skated, coached, and bicycled; she hasn't a needle or a thread about her in all the fifty-two toilettes so far found for her by collectors. Her wardrobe is all action. (And when she is not engaged in an active sport, she must be changing her costume!)

The *Boston Globe* Forbes Doll

In the nineties the *Boston Globe* newspaper also began to carry paper dolls, a practice that continued for decades. These dolls of the nineties represented a variety of subjects, and many were lithographed by Forbes Lithographing (illustrated). The unusual method of putting dolls together and of adding clothes to the doll in a weaving of slots and tabs is unique to this company. When

The Boston Herald *Lady was also the* Chicago Record *Lady. Her "toilettes" appeared in both papers weekly from 1895-96.*
Chicago Historical Society photographs by Walter W. Krutz.

collectors discuss a Forbes doll, they are referring to this woven method of paper doll construction.

Imported German Dolls

Europe, in the 1870s to the 1890s, was still producing and publishing magnificent paper dolls. In the 1880s sheets of beautifully lithographed, embossed paper dolls representing the German royal family, the House of Hapsburg, the kaiser, kaiserin, prince, princesses, maid, and toys were produced. A similar production was made of the House of Windsor and the English royal family. A book could be devoted to illustrating these dolls; a collector is fortunate to own one.

The German firm, Littauer and Bauer, was responsible for the beautiful lithographed, embossed Dennison paper dolls from the 1880s, and they also made lovely jointed dolls to sell under their own name (illustrated). These dolls represented famous actresses of the period: Fritzi Scheff, Della Fox, Ellen Terry, Lilly Langtry, Julia Marlowe, Lillian Russell, Maxine Elliot, and Adeline Patty. They came in several sizes, with arms, legs, and heads to be assembled.

As with the Dennison dolls, the child did the creative costuming. This doll, from the collection of the Chicago Historical Society, is, I think, a particularly interesting example. She is beautifully dated by her needlework samples and her Garfield ribbon. These dolls were so popular, paper lore tells us they were advertised even in the *Police Gazette*.

Besides the actress paper dolls, of which there were two styles,

Boston Herald Lady. "Toilettes" identified by Barbara Whitton Jendricks in Paper Dolls and Paper Toys. *Left to right: January 12, 1896; September 15, 1895; September 8, 1895; April 7, 1895; January 15, 1896; October 13, 1895; July 28, 1895; October 27, 1895; July 21, 1895.*

Boston Herald *Lady's ''toilettes.''* *Left to right: Doll: August 4, 1895; date unknown; date unknown; September 22, 1895; August 18, 1895.*
Doll: October 20, 1895; June 23, 1895; May 5, 1895; date unknown; date unknown. Chicago Historical Society photograph by Walter W. Krutz.

German embossed baby and nurse. **$75.** Courtesy of Cynthia Musser

bloomer or ballet, Littauer and Bauer also sold black baby dolls, with laughing face or smiling face; babies, smiling or crying; a peasant girl and a peasant boy; and an old man and lady. This company continued printing until World War II, when it was closed by Hitler. Merrimac Publishing, of New York, has reproduced a Littauer and Bauer jointed doll. It makes a nice contemporary addition to the collection and begs to be costumed.

72

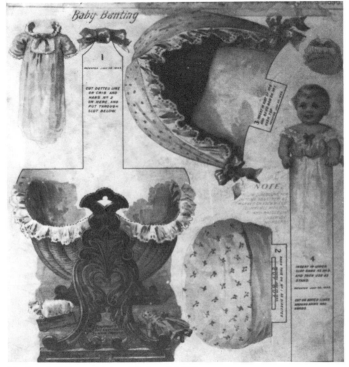

Forbes doll from Boston Globe. **$4.50** Addison Collection

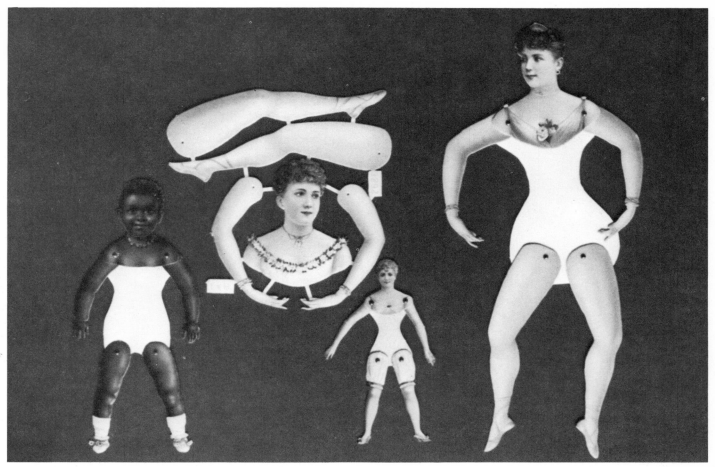

Littauer and Bauer dolls. They came in a multitude of sizes. Here are
9" black baby, unassembled doll, small 6½" Lillian Russell, 14" Lilly Langtry. **$10, each.**

Photographs by Walter W. Krutz, Chicago Historical Society

Littauer and Bauer treasure.

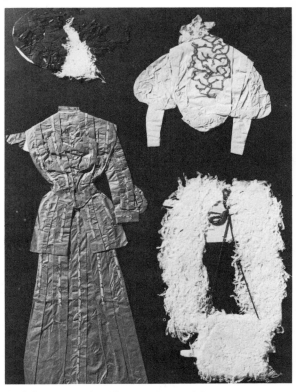

Stylish costumes for Chicago Historical Society Lady.

Cutwork needlepoint and Garfield banner add to charm of this wonderful doll. Chicago Historical Society, photograph by Walter W. Krutz.

My Lady Betty. Tuck doll, with characteristic flower-form dress. $40.

Raphael Tuck and Sons Company, Ltd.

The important publisher Raphael Tuck, "by appointment to her Majesty Queen Elizabeth II, Fine Art Publishers, London," not only published some of collectors' favorite paper dolls, but is also responsible for many of our favorite traditions—the Christmas card, the scenic postcard, and the valentine.

The firm began in 1866, when Raphael and Ernestine Tuck opened a small shop for the sale of pictures and frames. They prospered and entered the publishing field, printing chromolithographs, oleographs, and lithographs. They expanded and

opened offices in New York, London, and Paris. Their first paper doll was a baby with a nursing bottle, patented in 1893.

Unfortunately, in December, 1940, Raphael House, headquarters of the firm, was destroyed by German bombers, and all the records, early plates, and documents of Tuck history were lost. Once again it has been the lot of the collector to piece together paper doll history, and Barbara Whitton Jenricks, in

Winsome Winnie. Raphael Tuck. Note stylized flower-form costumes. $40.

Sweet Abigail. Raphael Tuck doll from Prince and Princess Series. $40.

Courtly Beatrice. Raphael Tuck. From Prince and Princess Series of dressing dolls (missing costume). **$40.**

Belle of the South. Raphael Tuck. **$50.**
Courtesy of Children's Museum of Indianapolis. Dolls not currently on exhibit.

The Maid of Honor. The Bridal Party Series. **$40.**

Paper Dolls and Paper Toys of Raphael Tuck and Sons, has issued a complete book on the subject.

For the collector it is helpful that all Tuck dolls have printed on the back, both the firm's identification, the easel-and-palette Tuck trademark, and the printed series name and number. It is also helpful for the collector to know that most Tuck dolls came with four costumes and four hats.

Early dolls are uniquely constructed. Their heads are separately cut and glued to a back tab. This caused the head to protrude slightly above the neck. Clothing has a high neck tab, which slips beneath the protruding head and holds the costume on. Dolls and costumes are made of sturdy card that contributes to the workability of this technique.

More often than not, Tuck sets are found and sold with mixed series costumes. The complete Lordly Lionel doll I quickly purchased with folder, dolls, and costumes turned out to be the box of Lionel and two Lionel costumes. The doll and the remainder of the costumes were Royal Reggie. This is typical. Tuck costumes were interchangeable, and the doll's owner played with her dolls as she pleased. Collectors can count themselves lucky to find any Tuck. In fact, child-order seems far happier and less stuffy than collector-classified; the mixed-up doll has "lived."

There is much confusion over the first dates of dolls. It is probably not of vital importance. The early dolls all belong to the 1890s. Dates can be estimated by notations (or significant lack of them) regarding the patent, 1894; the expansion of offices of the Tuck firms; and the fashion and art style of the dolls.

Tuck dolls were produced in series of series, and it seems to me that illustrating samplings of them is clearest if dolls of the nineties are divided into two groups: those reflecting the "English style," the Art Nouveau influence, and those reflecting the period life and style, which is probably from late 1898 on.

Tuck dolls of "English style" show the influence of the well-known illustrator of the period, Walter Crane. In 1884 he founded the English Art Workers Guild. In 1889, with his help, the Arts and Crafts Exhibition Society and the Guild of Handicrafts were started. These organizations themselves were influenced by William Morris and the Arts and Crafts Movement of 1861. The artists were reacting against the Industrial Age and Victorian materialism, the popular love of the machine-made "more" that piled tidies, antimacassars, screens, and aspidistras into parlors already filled with bric-a-brac, horsehair sofas, flowers, and fringed scarves.

Signatures of the Art Nouveau artistic style were the curving line, natural form, Japanese spatial concepts, and a love of Medievalism. Conjecture leads one to believe that the first Tuck paper dolls published under the meaningful heading Artistic Series meant to reflect the Art Nouveau style, and that this accounts for their beautifully stylized costumes. Further conjecture indicates that the artist Marguerite McDonald, whose name is found on the folders of the Prince and Princess dolls and the Belles Series must be a well known artist-illustrator of the English group dedicated to the principles of Art Nouveau.

This is, of course, conjecture. Nevertheless, it is clearly evident that flower forms unify all the costumes of the dolls in this group. Dresses are daffodils. Skirts are belled corollas. Collars, capes, and ruffles flare like petals and sepals. Sleeves puff into blossoms, and all is designed with a simplicity of form that is not typically Victorian.

Sets of English style, Artistic Series, include the following:

Our Pets Dressing Series. Dolly Delight, Winsom Winnie (illustrated), My Lady Betty (illustrated), and My Lady Edith.

Dolls for the Seasons Series. Dear Dorothy, Merry Marion, and Sweet Alice.

Prince and Princess Series. Royal Reggie, Lordly Lionel, Sweet Abigail, and Courtly Beatrice (illustrated).

Belles Series. Belle of the South, Belle of the West, Belle of Newport, and Belle of Saratoga.

The Bridal Party Series. The Bride 600, The Bridegroom 601, The Maid of Honor 602 (illustrated), and The Bridesmaid 603.

Fairytale Series. Mother Goose, Cinderella (illustrated), and Prince Charming (illustrated).

The Artistic Series also included dolls that were not done in the English art style of the period. Of course, they are exquisitely made too, and beautifully reflect the interests of the day.

One such series is called Dainty Dollies. It is of this period, but is not captioned Artistic Series. These dolls include Gentle Gladys, Fair Frances (illustrated), and Lovely Lillian (illustrated).

Most exciting to celebrity collectors is the Tuck Favorite Faces Series of the late 1890s, which showed actresses in costumes from their celebrated roles. Detailed from Barbara Witton Jenrick's *Paper Dolls of Raphael Tuck and Sons*, they are:

Ada Rehan as Katherine, *Taming of the Shrew*; Olivia,

Lovely Lilly. Tuck. Dainty Dollies Series. 9". $40.

Twelfth Night; Lady Teazel, *School for Scandal*; and Mistress Ford, *Merry Wives of Windsor*.

Julia Marlowe (illustrated) as Barbara Fritchie; Colinette; Constance, *Love Chase*; and Rosalind, *As You Like It*.

Mrs. Leslie Carter in *The Heart of Maryland*; Zaza.

Miss Maude Adams as Dorothy, *Christopher, Jr.*; Juliet, *Romeo and Juliet*; Lady Babbie, *The Little Minister*; and Gypsy, *The Little Minister*.

Prince Charming. The Fairytale Series. Dick Whittington, Prince, Little Boy Blue, Little Jack Horner, Prince Charming. **$40.**

Julia Marlowe. Tuck. Famous Faces Series. **$80.**

Courtesy, Henry Francis du Pont Winterthur Museum, Joseph Downs Manuscript Collection/
The Maxine Waldron Collection of Children's and Paper Toys

II. Nostalgia
The Turn of the Century 1910–1920

Nostalgia is subjective. To our grandfathers, it was the Ohio River, the Domino Club, and fat red strawberries in creamy, homemade ice cream. To me, it is Maine, ocean-sprayed rock, my dad, periwinkles, and a long, bamboo pole. For the purposes of this book, nostalgia begins in the sepia-toned turn of the century in the year 1901, when the gas lights dim and electricity flickers on. Telephones are cranking up, and white porcelain bathtubs impress the neighborhood. Queer contraptions called electric cabs and steamcars honk to herald the beginning of the automobile age. It is an exciting time. Queen Victoria is dead at eighty-two. Long live King Edward! McKinley has just been assassinated; Teddy Roosevelt is president. A new era has begun.

Paper dolls are still in style, but their fashions are changing. During the first decade skirts shorten, and it is the length of skirts that collectors need to know from 1900 on.

The S curve was the popular shape for the female at the beginning of the century. Skirts were long. The French designer Paul Poiret introduced the natural shape for the female. The skirt in 1910 was still floor-length; after 1905, the hobble skirt was introduced, and it incorporated an empire waist and draped skirt. The first world war changed and freed fashion. Waists, which had been high, reverted to the natural waist; skirts became full and rose to the ankle. Collars reached to the ears, and hats were inspired by the military.

In the twenties the illusion of a decade of flappers in short skirts and plunging necklines is only half true. The skirt was not short until 1926. Clothing in the era was tubular, however; waists were low, necks were plunging, busts were flat and boyish, bandeaux and long beads were popular. The cloche appeared in 1923, causing hair first to be bobbed and then shingled.

By the thirties waists and busts were back. Suits, small hats with veils, costume jewelry, fur jackets, padded shoulders, and strapless evening gowns were fashion news in the forties. In 1947, the Dior New Look appeared, lengthening hems and filling out skirts. Peplums, short jackets, and femininity were in.

The sixties went wild with minis, modis, tights, and psychedelic colors. The pants suit solved the problem for those who disliked the short hem. Long skirts were worn for evening. The hemline ceased to play an important fashion role in 1970 when the midi hemline failed to succeed, though designers pushed it.

Men's Fashions

From the Saalfield files at Kent State University comes this correspondence, pertaining to the 1939 paper doll book *Hollywood Fashion,* between the editor of Saalfield and the book's co-artist Corrine Bailey. The editor writes that she is

> delighted to hear you say . . . colorful . . . men's costumes will contribute a great deal of the splash. That's good. In most doll books the men and their costumes drag down rather than lift up the book. . . . Pardon me for saying this, but I have long felt it the truth, and if the Baileys can accomplish exactly the opposite, hats off to them, I say!

The Baileys did accomplish colorful male costumes in this book, and they did it by including lots of sports costumes. What can one do with gray flannel suits?

The Sunshine Doll. Male fashions have not changed radically in the twentieth century. $10.   Courtesy of Cynthia Musser

Illustrated here is a 1910 newspaper Sunshine Doll, a handsome and debonair gentleman. He could just as well be a 1980 gentleman. There have been no enormous changes over the years in male suits. Most fashion news seems to consist of such earth-shattering change as going from two buttons, thin lapels, and thin ties to three buttons, fat lapels, and fat ties.

The exception to this is, of course, the introduction of the leisure suit, which appeared in the 1970s, and which some men wore to the office. These were almost an adoption of the Norfolk jacket with trousers. Counterculture and young men wore nonuniform garb in the 1960s and the early 1970s; blue jeans were the youthful uniform in the sixties and seventies. Big bell-bottom pants and pinched-waist, flared coats were the style in the sixties. In the 1930s knickers were popular for sport; zoot suits appeared for Damon Runyonesque characters in the forties. The sport shirt appeared in early century.

Sport jackets have always given men the chance to show some style, but even these have tended to be somber plaids, herringbones, and tweeds. The sixties had a lasting influence on style, and men's sport and leisure clothing has tended to be more colorful since then. Colored shirts are now the norm. Ruffled, colored shirts in pastels and varying shades of dinner jackets are worn. Sport jackets and sport pants are now bright colors or pastels in checks, plaids, patchworks, or paisleys. Splendor may be coming back, and male attire will lift up paper doll books again.

From the 1900s children's clothing was designed especially for them. They no longer emulated Father and Mother. As a result, I find it much more difficult to date children's styles. From 1900 to 1920, dresses had low waists, belts or sashes, and skirts were short. Shoes are a major aid to identification. High-button boots with stockings were worn in the early 1900s to the 1910s.

From the 1920s middy suits, Russian tunics with pleated skirts, and jumpers with blouses were popular for little girls. In the thirties, classic suits, smocked dresses, and Shirley Temple dresses were worn. Party dresses were always a part of the child's wardrobe. They were ribboned, ruffled, and flowered. From 1910 through 1930 they might have come from Paris.

From the forties to now, skirts, blouses, sweaters, shirtdresses, jumpers, jackets, and pants (slacks and jeans) have continued as children's wear. In the sixties, styles for children incorporated the mini, tights, and bright psychedelic and pop art fabrics.

In the early 1900s boys wore sailor suits, Russian tunics, and Buster Brown tunics with wide collars and black scarves. From 1900 to 1910 black stockings were worn with laced boots or oxfords. Caps and sailor hats were popular.

From 1910 rompers and short pants that buttoned to shirts made practical styles for little boys. Older boys wore knee pants. Eton suits, short jackets, and short pants in flannel, with knee socks, brass buttons, and caps became a lasting classic in the 1930s. Corduroy knickers, knitted vests, knee socks, high-laced boots with flaps for pocket knives, caps, and Norfolk jackets were worn by schoolboys in the 1930s. School-aged boys wore short pants in the thirties and forties. By the fifties, long pants were worn by all school-aged boys. Jeans and corduroys were worn for everyday. Leisure suits were worn by boys in the seventies. Sport coats were worn from the forties to today.

Commercial Publishers

Selchow and Richter. This seems a fitting publisher with which to begin a new century. It is not known when they began publication of paper dolls in New York City; their output is relatively small. However, my favorite paper doll, the one I do not own and covet most, is their Teddy Bear, a replica of the toy sensation of 1903.

Bears were toys in the nineteenth century, but they were animal toys, the type one pulled on a string or loaded in an ark. The Teddy Bear of 1903 was a completely different sort of bear. He had personality; he was lovable, huggable, and the toy to take to bed. His creation has been claimed both by the German firm

Teddy Bear. Selchow and Richter. **$75.** Courtesy of Cynthia Musser

Lady Betty. Selchow and Richter. **$50.** Courtesy of Cynthia Musser

of Steiff who showed a stuffed bear in the 1904 Toy Fair in Leipzig and by the American Ideal Toy Company.

Morris Michton, founder of Ideal, was inspired by a 1903 *Washington Post* cartoon of President Teddy Roosevelt on a hunt sparing a bear cub. Michton decided to create a stuffed bear. He gave his bear cute button eyes, a round, cuddly shape, and obtained permission from the president to call his new toy Teddy's Bear.

The success of both the Ideal bear and the Steiff bear was phenomenal. Naturally, paper doll manufacturers turned out teddy bears, too.

Merrimac Publishing has reproduced this teddy bear in tiny size for a contemporary collector.

Decalo Litho. Penny-graphics, printed in flat, primary colors from simple line drawings, the Decalo Litho paper doll sheets, as illustrated, make fascinating, provocative additions to a collection. I am indebted to Joyce McLellan for the paper lore title of these dolls, The Women's Suffrage Set, and it is entertaining to see the progression of the female from one set to another. Personal interpretations of these dolls lead to most revealing conversations. What do you think?

Schoolgirl. Raphael Tuck. **$40.** Addison Collection

The Women's Suffrage Set. Decalo Litho. **$10.**

Artful Alice. Little Darlings Series. **$55.**
Courtesy of Children's Museum of Indianapolis. Dolls not currently on exhibit.

Raphael Tuck. This company was still publishing beautiful paper dolls in the 1900s. The schoolgirl doll illustrated is unidentified by series, and seems to have been published individually. Three other dolls of similar period and size have turned up. They most likely date from late 1890 to early 1900. The charming Artful Alice (illustrated) dates after 1910.

McLoughlin Brothers. They continued to dominate the field of children's books until 1920, when several family deaths caused the sale of the company to Milton Bradley of Springfield, Massachusetts. Paper dolls from this period included the series, Elegant New Paper Doll, which included Grace Green (illustrated), Nellie North (illustrated), and Karl King.

Grace Green. McLoughlin. $45.
Courtesy of Children's Museum of Indianapolis. Dolls not currently on exhibit.

Nellie North. McLoughlin. $45.
Courtesy of Children's Museum of Indianapolis. Dolls not currently on exhibit.

Beatrice. Woolworth doll. $45. Courtesy of Cynthia Musser

Saalfield. In 1900 Arthur J. Saalfield bought the publishing department of the Werner Company of Akron, Ohio, and the Saalfield Publishing Company was born. The firm began printing dictionaries and Bibles. It went on to publishing children's series like Billy Whiskers, Auto Boys, and Campfire Girls, and it developed a line of popular cloth books for small children. Sensing the need for less expensive books for the chain stores that

were appearing, Mr. Saalfield brought out a less expensive, smaller, child's book. The first paper dolls were done in 1918, Dollies To Cut and Paint.

Woolworth Dolls. Tall dolls appeared in glassine envelopes in the Woolworth stores in this period, and are considered a wonderful specialty. They are being researched as they appear by collectors.

Newspaper Dolls

Boston Post: **Polly's Paper Playmates.** Polly and her chums are dear, but it's Sister Prue who makes this series so perfect. Richly drawn with elegant detail and printed in beautiful color, Polly's Paper Playmates are to my mind the most desirable of news supplement dolls. These were run in 1910–1911.

Polly. Polly's Paper Playmates. $18. Addison Collection

Sister Prue at the Costume Ball. $18. Addison Collection

Sister Prue on Charles Street. Polly's Paper Playmates. **$18.**
Addison Collection

The Sunshine Paper Dolls. A briefer, but equally delightful, series of newspaper paper dolls was run in both the *Boston American* and the *Buffalo Express* in 1916. The series consisted of the stylish Sunshine family and nursery tales, run on this schedule:

Martha	November 14, 1915
Peter	November 21, 1915
Mrs. Patience	November 7, 1915

Baby Bob	November 28, 1915
Father, George Washington	December 5, 1915
Little Bo-Peep	December 12, 1915
Little Boy Blue	December 19, 1915
Peter Pumpkin	December 26, 1915

Boston Globe. The *Boston Globe* nearly always ran a paper doll. In 1910 the family was drawn by Miss Bertha Capen. From 1907 to 1908 the *Boston Globe* ran a teddy bear in their news supplement. Published weekly, the bear had costumes including a golf suit, a yachting suit, a pirate suit, a jockey suit, a college gown, a blacksmith suit, a Continental uniform, a Roughrider suit, and an automobile suit.

Magazine Dolls

The great continuing popularity of the paper doll led to the inclusion of dolls in almost every family newspaper and magazine during the first thirty years of the 1900s. Dolls were so numerous it would be impossible to illustrate them all. Included here, therefore, are the magazine dolls most desired by collectors.

Beginning in the *Ladies' Home Journal* of October, 1908, Sheila Young introduced Miss Lettie Lane, whose paper doll family and friends decorated *Journal* pages until July, 1915, when Lettie gracefully introduced Betty Bonnet and her friends, family, and toys.

Both Lettie's and Betty's families have most collectible weddings, and Lettie's newly married sister, presumably on an around-the-world honeymoon, sent Lettie magnificent travel paper doll pictures from afar (illustrated).

Mother, Sunshine Family. **$10.**

Lettie Lane Around the World. **$15.**

Betty Bonnet. **$15.**

Most notably and collectibly, Betty Bonnet's childhood spans World War I, and all male doll costumes of the series at this time include World War I uniforms (illustrated).

Sheila Young also drew paper doll delights for *Good Housekeeping.* Polly Pratt and her family, friends, and toys appeared in the magazine from 1919 to 1921.

The beloved and irresistible Dolly Dingle of Dingle Dell, drawn by Grace C. Drayton, enchanted generations of yesterday's children. Known for drawing the Campbell Soup Kids and for her signature, a graphic H-smile in a round cherubic face, Drayton introduced Dolly Dingle in *Pictorial Review* in March, 1913, with a miniseries of Dolly, Billy Bumps, Kitty Cutie, and Frisky Fido.

They reappeared in March, 1916, and Drayton continued until 1933 with only one interruption—1925–1926, the Bobbs series. Dolly Dingle traveled around the world several times, patriotically supported World War I, and even turned opera buff. In 182 appearances, she never lost her smile, though in 1926 she lost some color, aging cheerily in two tones of green and red.

Rose O'Neill coined the word *kewpish* in the second decade of the 1900s. *Kewpish* meant cute, and her little cherubs, sprinkled on the story pages of *The Woman's Home Companion,* were cute.

Begun at first as an illustrated moralistic, rhymed story page for children, the paper dolls seemed to occur spontaneously in

Betty Bonnet went to a wedding. **$15.**

Betty Bonnet. The series is a good source of World War I uniforms. **$15.**

Billy Bumps, Dolly Dingle's friend. **$15.**

Kewpie. By Rose O'Neill, Woman's Home Companion. **$15.**

1912. From them the first Kewpie doll evolved. This was the first doll-birth in paper doll history. (Barbie was the *big* second.)

In 1903 Edwin Porter, a cameraman in the studios of Thomas A. Edison, inspired by the fantasy films of Frenchman George Meles and bored with moving scenic views and newsreels, produced two dramatic movie episodes, the second of which was *The Great Train Robbery.* It was the first box office sensation and began the movie industry, America's biggest medium of mass entertainment until television.

Perhaps the first series to represent movie stars as paper dolls was run in *Ladies World,* in 1916 through 1918. In part it

Mary Pickford	September, 1916
Billie Burke	October, 1916
Marguerite Clark	November, 1916
Anita Stewart	December, 1916
Shirley Mason	January, 1917
Marie Doro	February, 1917
George Le Guere	March, 1917
Charlotte Walker	April, 1917
Mary Miles Minter	May, 1917
Pauline Frederick	June, 1917
Charlie Chaplin	July, 1917

Waiting for the show. The Columbia Theatre, Bowling Green, Kentucky, 1911. From newsreels and scenic views to features, stars, and paper dolls. Photographed at Kentucky Library, Western Kentucky University.

In 1917 *Delineator Magazine* presented a guessing contest with paper dolls as clues. The prize was $50, and there were six contests. Mystery paper dolls were:

Mary Pickford and Douglas Fairbanks	March, 1917
Francis X. Bushman and Marguerite Clark	April, 1917
E. H. Sothern and Geraldine Farrar	May, 1917
Pauline Frederick and Earle Williams	(date not known)
William Farnum and Geraldine Farrar	
(date not known, experts disagree on identity)	
Thelma Salter, Bobby Connelly and	
Mary McAlister	August, 1917

The Ladies' World *movie dolls, 1916–18.* **$15.**

The Delineator *magazine's "Who Are They?" feature.* **$12.**

The Twenties

F. Scott Fitzgerald termed it "The Jazz Age." Shieks and shebas shimmied, blackbottomed, and Charlestoned. Painted vamps smoked and sipped hootch from rumrunners and bootleggers in snazzy speakeasys. Youth was flaming; and Mother and Father were old sports, who did the crosswords, played mahjongg, or took in a Valentino, Chaplin, or Fairbanks movie.

Some worried about stocks bought on margin, land sales in Florida, or the scandals of Teapot Dome, but Bix Beiderbecke blew and crystal radio sets blared "Japanese Sandman." Besides, there were heroes to cheer: Babe Ruth, Red Grange, and Charles Lindbergh. These years were called the "Whoopee Years" and the "Roaring Twenties," and paper dolls captured some of the gaiety. Of course, Polly Pratt and Dolly Dingle stayed responsibly straight, and McLoughlin Brothers and Dennison continued to publish stable, wholesome paper dolls. It was in the movie paper dolls that the madness and color of the twenties was apparent.

Movie Dolls

There were Jumbo Movy-Dols in 1920, *Photoplay* favorites with copyright held by Percy Reeves (illustrated). Mary Miles Minter, Marguerite Clark, Mary Pickford, and Lila Lee were all wonderful large "dols." They were all ingenues, sweethearts of the silent screen, and they are wonderfully collectible today.

Photoplay Magazine, in 1919–1920, also published a more extensive series of smaller Movy-Dols, with Mary Pickford, Elsie

Ferguson, Norma Talmadge, Charlie Chaplin, Geraldine Farrar, May Allison, Marguerite Clark, and Douglas Fairbanks. These dolls were so popular they were even printed on school writing tablets! Instead of passing notes and dodging spitballs, young schoolgirls of the twenties must have snipped out screen stars and pantomimed scenes from *The Four Horsemen of the Apocalypse.*

In 1925 the *Woman's Home Companion* did a short series of four Movie Children Cut-Outs. In May there was Jackie Coogan; in June, Baby Peggy; in July, Peter Pan; and in October, Our Gang.

Also in 1925 a rare and highly sought series, Hollywood Dollies, appeared. They were sheets of sturdy card sold in glassine envelopes in series. There were at least sixty-six stars and each had three movie-related costumes. The list of stars included Rudolph Valentino, Tom Mix, Colleen Moore, Norma Shearer, Nita Naldi, Hoot Gibson, Mary Astor, Francis X. Bushman, and Rin Tin Tin.

Magazine Dolls

My favorite flapper paper doll is Bonnie Bobbs (illustrated). Orpha Klinker is the artist, and her short four-doll series appeared in the *Woman's Home Companion* in 1925, when Grace Drayton interrupted her Dolly Dingle series. The four

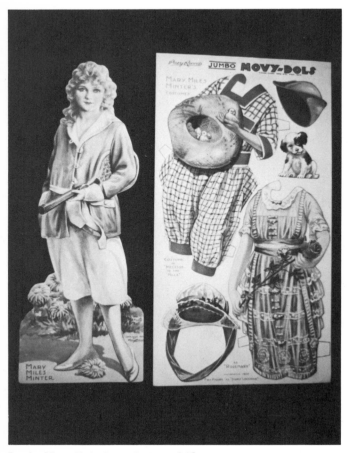

Jumbo Movy-Dol. Percy Reeves. **$45.** Courtesy of Cynthia Musser

Movy-Dol. Elsie Ferguson. **$30.** Addison Collection

dolls in the series were:

Introducing Betty Bobbs	January
Betty Bobbs's Baby Brother, Buddy Bobbs	February
Betty Bobbs's Older Sister, Bonnie Bobbs	May
Betty Bobbs's Older Brother, Bobby Bobbs	July

Katherine Shane also captured the style and Deco feeling of the twenties in a wonderful series, which ran briefly in the *Woman's Home Companion.* In this series were:

Madeline of Maine	September, 1926
Texas Tom	November, 1926
Winifred of Wisconsin	February, 1927
Carl of California	April, 1927
Katy of Kentucky	June, 1927

The McCall Family series of paper dolls is also noted for its Deco paper doll style. These were drawn by Nandor Honti and appeared in *McCall's* in 1925–1926:

Mrs. McCall and Little Betty	September, 1925
Master McCall and Sister Nell	October, 1925
Sister Nell Goes to a Party	November, 1925
The Twins Make a New Year's Call	January, 1926
Baby McCall Goes for a Ride	March, 1926
Two Jolly Playmates Romp in the Park	April, 1926
A Boudoir Doll	May, 1926
Boudoir Furniture	June, 1926
Boudoir Furniture	July, 1926

Bonnie Bobbs. *She makes a perfect flapper. Drawn by Orpha Klinker for* Pictorial Review. **$10.**

Peter Pan. Woman's Home Companion, *1925.* **$8.**
Courtesy of Children's Museum of Indianapolis. Dolls not currently on exhibit.

Betty Bobbs. 1925. **$10.**

Nandor Honti Deco dolls, McCall's; Delineator *(1921); Jessie Louise Taylor, The Mexican Twins,* Ladies' Home Journal *(1922).* **$8.**

Commercial Dolls

Of course, much of the twenties' color comes from writers like Fitzgerald and cartoonists like John Held, who reveled in the fads and foibles of the time. Will Rogers said, ''One-third of America promotes; two-thirds of America provides,'' and though the divorce rate was up, traditional family values and childrearing practices were still the norm. Most of America lived on the farm or in a small town, and paper dolls in general reflect these little girls and their families.

McLoughlin Brothers. In the 1920s McLoughlin was sold to its competitor, Milton Bradley of Springfield, Massachusetts, and Bradley moved the company there. Three paper doll books were produced: Nursery Rhyme Party Dolls; Our Dollies and How to Dress Them (boxed, reproduced by Merrimac); and a book with two names, Wild World of Costume Dolls and The New Model Book of Dolls. Both contained the same dolls.

Raphael Tuck. The darling Our Bonnie Series of Dressing Dolls was issued by Tuck at this time, and it included Bonnie Bessie, Bonnie Billy, and Bonnie Betty.

Katherine Shane captured Deco in this series in Woman's Home Companion. **$10.**

New Model Book of Dolls. *McLoughlin.* **$35.** Addison Collection.

Foreign costumes from New Model Book of Dolls. Addison Collection

Edna, New Model Book of Dolls. Addison Collection

Ethel, New Model Book of Dolls. Addison Collection

Foreign costumes from New Model Book of Dolls. Addison Collection

Foreign costumes from New Model Book of Dolls. Addison Collection

Foreign costumes from New Model Book of Dolls. Addison Collection

Dennison. Since their appearance in the 1880s, the Dennison paper dolls with clothes to be created by the child were popular. Illustrated is a set from the twenties. The accompanying booklet states that the "new dolls are a wonderful improvement over the ones that for many years have come from the other side. They are American in face and dress and true reproductions of our own children." The other side, of course, refers to Germany, a country most unpopular after World War I. The boxed sets of dolls, patterns, and materials sold for fifty cents. Individual dolls could be purchased at the following prices: Baby, five cents; Little Girl, six cents; and Older girl, seven cents.

Milton Bradley. Milton Bradley also issued a darling dress-designing paper doll in the twenties, Bradley's Tru-Life Paper Dolls, which contained materials for the child to use in creating her own doll dresses. The dolls, however, were not jointed.

Whitman. In 1907 E. H. Wadewitz began the Western Publishing Company in Racine, Wisconsin. It became Whitman in 1915. Wadewitz began with a second-hand press. Today the firm is the largest producer of children's books in the country (Little Golden books) and is combined with other firms like Dell and Mattel.

The company entered the paper doll field in the late 1920s, largely through the efforts of Samuel Lowe, who in the forties left Whitman and formed his own paper doll company. Lowe discovered Queen Holden, who drew Whitman paper doll books for twenty years. Her beautiful paper doll books form a collection specialty in themselves. Baby Joan was Queen Holden's first doll book, and Whitman's best seller in 1929. Baby Brother and Baby Sister were also produced in that same year.

Platt and Nourse Company—Platt and Munk Company. The Platt and Nourse Company published several paper doll books in 1920. During this decade, Platt left Nourse and joined Munk, establishing the Platt and Munk Company, which still produces many lovely books.

Woolworth. Woolworth dolls were also published during this decade.

Platt and Nourse. **$20.** Addison Collection

Platt and Nourse. **$20.** Addison Collection

Dennison. Still popular creative doll set. **$35.**

Dennison dolls with American faces.

Dennison instruction booklet.

Clever trunk package of Betty Is Going Away to Boarding School. Samuel Gabriel Sons. **$40.**

Betty Is Going Away to Boarding School. Samuel Gabriel Sons.

Courtesy of Cynthia Musser

91

The Stylish Thirties

On Black Thursday, October 29, 1929, the stock market crashed and the Great Depression began. Hoover told the country there was nothing to fear, but by 1932, 10,000 people were out of jobs, banks had failed, and factories were closed. Thousands were homeless. Hoovervilles, shantytowns, huddled across the country, and the homeless slept under "Hoover blankets"—newspapers. There were breadlines and soup kitchens. The economic picture was grim, but movies and paper dolls flourished. They had three things in common: they were cheap; they offered entertainment and provided escape; and they did it with style.

A movie ticket cost twenty-five cents, and it bought a double feature and often an additional treat like bingo, keeno, and screeno. Dish night, bank night, and organ recitals also kept the theaters full. Paper doll books were a good buy, too. They cost a dime at the chains; Kresge, Grant, and Woolworth, and they afforded hours of wonderful play—a welcome fact in hard times.

Queen Holden Dolls. Holden's paper dolls drawn for Whitman were beautiful. Her Baby Nancy, a shape book, was produced in three different versions over the years. The first, in 1931, sold over 10,000 copies and established a paper doll record.

Beautiful babies were one of Holden's specialties. She did Baby Jean, the Dy-Dee doll, and Baby Betty. They were more than just lovable. They had all the paraphernalia babies need: bassinets, carriages, playpens, washtubs, bath powder, baby oil, bottles, teething rings, rubber ducks, and roly-polys. Little girls could really play mother!

Families were another Holden specialty. My favorite (illustrated) came with a vintage automobile and a *nursemaid!* This was Depression time! In total, Holden drew thirty-six books for Whitman in the 1930s, and she was instrumental in their early success.

Paper Doll Family. Drawn by Queen Holden. **$50.**
Reprinted by permission of Western Publishing Company, Inc.

Paper Doll Family Game, complete with maid.

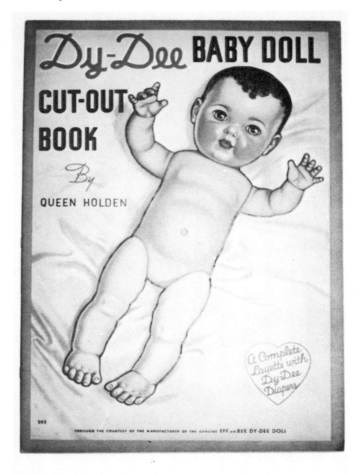

Dy-Dee doll, sensation of the thirties. Whitman. **$35.**
Courtesy of EFFANBEE Doll Corporation

Movie Star Dolls. The first movie star celebrity book was Movie Star Paper Dolls. It was drawn by Holden and included stars Clara Bow, Sue Carol, Anita Page, and Claudette Colbert.

In 1938 people hummed "Someday My Prince Will Come," and Father tramped to the office singing "Heigh Ho, Heigh Ho, It's Off to Work We Go." *Snow White* was at the theater, Walt Disney's first feature-length animated cartoon. The movie took four years to make and consisted of 477,000 photographs of drawings done by 570 artists. *Snow White* was total enchantment, and so were the paper dolls.

The thirties were the years of the child movie star, and Shirley Temple was the queen moppet. Early in the decade, Albert

Saalfield contracted with the child to produce her paper doll, coloring books, storybooks, and so on. Shirley Temple was the country's darling, and eight Shirley Temple paper dolls were published during the thirties. Some are illustrated. (See Movie Star Books from the 1930s in this chapter.)

The dolls were designed and drawn by artists Bill and Corrine Bailey, and this pair was to Saalfield's success as Holden was to Whitman's. Beginning with Shirley, the Baileys developed a new system for creating the doll from an underdeveloped negative, working up to a true likeness of the star.

Hollywood Fashion Dolls. The Saalfield archives at Kent State University Library in Ohio contain correspondence between Alta L. Taylor, editor, and Corrine Bailey, artist, pertaining to Hollywood Fashion Dolls. I always knew this was an especially stylish set of paper dolls, and now I know why. Style was spelled *swank!*

Negotiating the price of the artwork, Corrine Bailey wrote of the asking price of $600, high for the thirties, that she ''cannot consider a penny less. . . . SWANK is desired and SWANK never was cheap—what?''

Price agreed upon, Taylor, on January 21, 1939, wrote to Bailey:

> I note you say . . . 12 or 14 pieces to a costume page and they will just ''revel'' in swank! Good! Study your styles from the most sophisticated fashions, and then overdo those a ''wee'' bit. Fill in every bit of space you can—crowd in such things as bottles of perfume from the smartest shops—showing ostrich plumes done in glass, etc., etc. . . . Put in short, shoulder fur garments, boleros to be worn over dresses, purses, gloves, swanky furred galoshes; the present built-up platform shoes, and all that truck; skiis, ice skates, riding crops, and the paraphernalia of the ultra set. . . . You see in all of this the gist of the talk in Mr. Saalfield's office.

The work was begun. Bailey wrote in February that she was using back numbers of *Esquire, Harper's,* and *Photoplay* for the men. She also inquired if it were

permissible to use just swimming trunks without uppers on some of our men figures? These days one seldom sees a man in anything but the trunks. However, we thought it best to consult you and save possible grief. . . . How about cigarettes and pipes? . . . Both boys and girls? . . . Please answer immediately. . . .

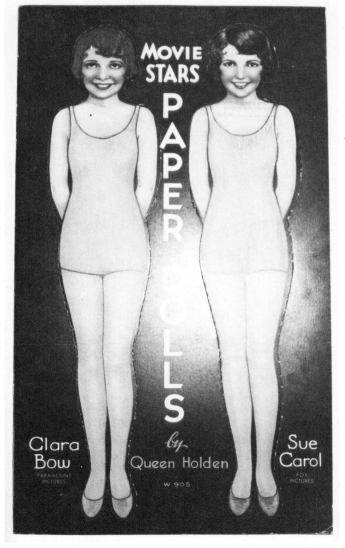

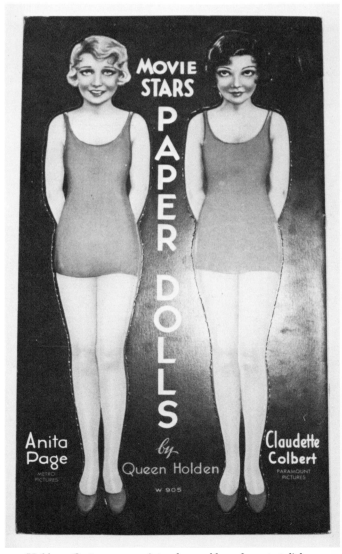

Movie Stars. The first celebrity movie star paper doll book. Drawn by Queen Holden. Costumes were interchangeable and most stylish. **$50 and up.** Reprinted by permission of Western Publishing Company, Inc.

Movie Stars. The first celebrity movie star paper doll book. Drawn by Queen Holden. Costumes were interchangeable and most stylish. **$50 and up.** Reprinted by permission of Western Publishing Company, Inc.

A Western Union telegram was sent February 6, 1939, in reply: "SHOW ONLY ONE MAN DOLL WITHOUT UPPERS TRUNKS ONLY STOP THIS DOLL MUST BE ON BACK COVER STOP NO CIGARETTES NO PIPES STOP. . . . WRITING."

A letter followed with the results of a conference with Mr. Saalfield: "Allow one man doll nude to the waist, which will allow you to show him in swim trunks only. However . . . this doll must be on the back cover. Regardless of both boys and girls now using cigarettes, no pipes and no liquor in the book."

Childhood was protected and cherished in the 1930s. The fun was still there, as you can see when Mrs. Bailey asked Alta Taylor to poll the editorial staff and select the "swankiest" names of the decade for the dolls. On January 27, 1939, Alta Taylor sent the lists:

Men		Women	
Tony	Peter	Lola	Barbara
Frederic	Jon (no *h*)	Dolores	Jeanne
Lucius	Michael	Vivian	Marilyn

With such attention to detail, it was no wonder these paper dolls had style!

Shirley Temple. She was the queen moppet of the 1930s.
Courtesy of Rand McNally and Company. Addison Collection.

Snow White. Drawn by Queen Holden for Whitman. **$50 and up.**
Reprinted by permission of Western Publishing Company, Inc. ©Walt Disney Productions.

Shirley Temple and Her Movie Costumes. Saalfield, #1773, 1938. **$60 and up.** Courtesy of Rand McNally and Company

Shirley Temple. Saalfield, #21112, 1934. **$60.**
Courtesy of Rand McNally and Company

Shirley Temple. Saalfield, #1761, 1937. **$60 and up.**

Hollywood Fashion Dolls. Saalfield, #2242, 1939. **$20.**
Courtesy of Rand McNally and Company

The Princess Paper Doll Book. The news story of the thirties was the abdication of King Edward VIII from the throne of England after a reign of only 325 days. He said, ''I have found it impossible to carry the heavy burden of responsibility and to discharge my duties as king . . . without the help and support of the woman I love.'' An American divorcee, Wallis Simpson, was the woman, and the Anglican Church would not accept a divorcee in the palace. King Edward became the Duke of Windsor, went into exile with his bride, and George VI became king.

Shirley Temple. Saalfield, #1715, 1935. **$60 and up.**

Style was spelled swank.

The Princess Paper Doll Book. Saalfield, #2216, 1939. **$60.**
Courtesy of Rand McNally and Company

Doll book commemorating the abdication of King Edward VIII and the coronation of King George VI.

Merrill Dolls. In 1934 Marion Merrill began the Merrill Publishing Company in Chicago, Illinois. With publishing expertise from the *Chicago Tribune* and *Liberty Magazine,* Merrill took the drafts of ten children's books to the well known Chicago printer, Regensteiner Corporation, hoping to form a business liaison.

Regensteiner was interested. They agreed that if Merrill could sell sample books to the chain stores, they would print them. Merrill met the challenge, sold the books, and signed a ten-year contract with Regensteiner. The Merrill Company was the country's second largest publisher of children's books from the thirties through the fifties.

Merrill books are probably first on the list for collectors of movie star paper doll books. Merrill paid enormous attention to the artwork, and Regensteiner, pioneer in three- and four-color printing, used beautiful inks. (Regensteiner also printed many lovely Saalfield books.) In 1944 the company name was changed from Merrill Publishing to Merrill Company at the acrimonious conclusion of the contract with Regensteiner, and Merrill took her business to a variety of printers.

Merrill died in 1978, and in 1979 Jean Woodcock purchased the company. Since then Woodcock has published one limited-edition paper doll, Vivien Leigh, by artist Marilyn Henry. Merrill would have been pleased with this paper doll. Collectors hope for more Woodcock-Henry paper dolls.

The first three paper dolls published by Merrill Publishing were Quintuplets, the Dionne Babies, 1935, M3488; Wedding of the Paper Dolls, 1935, M3497; and Sonja Henie, 1939 (illustrated).

Dionne Quintuplet Dolls. On May 28, 1934 five girls— Emilie, Yvonne, Cecile, Marie, and Annette—were born to Olivia and Elizire Dionne in Ontario, Canada. The world was thrilled. They were the only known set of quintuplets to survive childbirth, and Allan Roy Defoe, the attending physician was given the credit. During the thirties there were Dionne movies, dolls, coloring books, books, and paper dolls. Merrill and Whitman both published quintuplet paper dolls, and they rivaled Shirley Temple in popularity. (See Movie Star Books from the 1930s in this chapter.)

Samuel Gabriel Sons and Company. Beautiful, prized paper dolls from this company produced in the thirties included:
    Bridal Party
    Dollies a la Mode
    Little Americans from Many Lands
    Modern Dolls A Plenty
    The Costume Party—Betty Campbell
    Town and Country Paper Dolls
    Twinnies (small box)
    Twinnies (larger set with different dolls)
    Sisters
    Williamsburg Colonial Dress

Collectors cherish these beautiful 1930s Saalfield paper dolls. **$30 and up.** Courtesy of Rand McNally and Company

Sonja Henie.
Merrill, #3475, 1939.
$85 and up.
Courtesy of Merrill Co.,
Publishers (Jean Woodcock)

Sonja's sumptious styles.

Radio Dolls. In the early twenties, the radio was called the wireless. By the thirties, radio was mass entertainment. "Just Plain Bill," "Road of Life," "Lorenzo Jones," "Our Gal Sunday," and "Stella Dallas," were weekday serials at fifteen-minute intervals that enthralled housewives, while "Little Orphan Annie," "Terry and the Pirates," and "Jack Armstrong, All American Boy" brought the children scurrying home for dinner and secret decoder messages. Evenings in the thirties revolved around nightly favorites like Eddie Cantor, used to ask me, their fossil mother. The answer was, of course, "Paper dolls, I cut them out while I listened."

A few radio programs led to paper dolls. Some from the thirties and forties were:

Baby Snooks, Whitman (Queen Holden)
Charlie McCarthy, Whitman (Queen Holden)
Hour of Charm, Saalfield, 1943, 2481
Quiz Kids, Saalfield, 1942, 2430

Newspaper Dolls. Movie stars were popular as cutout features in newspapers in the thirties. The best known are probably from the *Chicago Tribune* and the *St. Louis Post-Dispatch*.

The *Chicago Tribune* series ran from 1936 to 1937. Some of the stars included were Olivia de Haviland, Gail Patrick, Ruby

The Costume Party. Gabriel dolls are collector prized today. Betty Campbell, artist. $40. Addison Collection

Dolls from The Costume Party illustrate the beautiful portrait paper dolls Betty Campbell is noted for. Addison Collection

Platt and Munk Dolls. The Platt and Munk Company published many charming boxed paper dolls during the thirties. A sampling is:

I'm Growing Up Dolls To Cut and Dress, 255A
Gladys de Beaulieu, 1937
Mary Lou and Her Friends
Playtime Dolls
Teddy Bear and His Friends to Dress, 1932, 222

Comic Strip Dolls. "See you in the funny papers" meant "see you later" in 1930. In 1905 comic strips separated from cartoons, and Bud Fischer established the first permanent daily long-run comic strip with characters Mutt and Jeff. By the 1920s comics were an important part of the paper and a large part of the Sunday specials.

Etta Kett, Bringing Up Father, Katzenjammer Kids, Winnie Winkle, Tillie the Toiler, Dixie Duggan, Jane Arden, Boots and Her Buddies, Flash Gordon, Jungle Jim, and Fritzi Ritz all had cutouts with their comics. These dolls are a specialty in themselves and it would take several books to discuss them all.

Charlie McCarthy, Baby Snooks, ''Inner Sanctum,'' Red Skeleton, and Kate Smith. ''What did you look at?'' my children Keeler, Virginia Wiedler, Ida Lupino, Rochelle Hudson, and Anita Louise.

The series from the *St. Louis Post-Dispatch* was the most extensive. George Conrey was the artist. Called Dressographs, they also included stars of the St. Louis Muni Opera. The *St. Louis Post-Dispatch* series ran from November 1, 1931, to 1936. It included 243 stars, including Spencer Tracy, Irene Dunne, Ruby Keeler, Baby LeRoy, James Cagney, Adolph Menjou, Edward Everett Horton, Alice Faye, Otto Kruger, Warner Baxter, Norma Shearer, Charles Laughton, Fred Astaire, Rosalind Russell, Noah Berry, Myrna Loy, Helen Hayes, Stan Laurel, Oliver Hardy, Shirley Temple, and Jane Withers.

Movie Star Books from the 1930s

1931:
Whitman
    900 Our Gang (Queen Holden)
    W905 Movie Stars (Anita Page, Claudette Colbert, Clara Bow, and Sue Carol) (Queen Holden)
1934:
Saalfield
    2112 Shirley Temple
1935:
Saalfield
    1715 Shirley Temple Standing Dolls
    1727 Shirley Temple Standing Doll
    1739 Shirley Temple and Her Playhouse

Merrill
    3488 Quintuplets, the Dionne Babies
Whitman
    998 Five Paper Dolls (Queen Holden and Dionne quintuplet pictures)
1936:
Whitman
    977 Jane Withers
    1055 Annette
    1055 Cecile
    1055 Emilie
    1055 Marie
    1055 Yvonne
Saalfield
    1756 Shirley Temple (34″)
1937:
Saalfield
    1761 Shirley Temple
1938:
Saalfield
    1773 Shirley Temple (movie wardrobe)
Whitman
    996 Jane Withers
Dell
    1938 Jane Withers
1939:
Merrill
    3475 Sonja Henie
Saalfield
    1782 Shirley Temple

Bridal Party.
Gabriel. **$40.**

Addison Collection

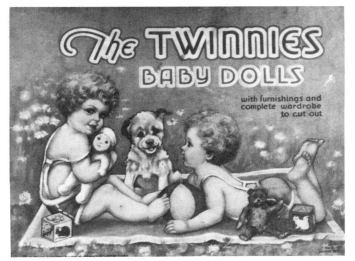

Twinnies. Gabriel. **$40.** Addison Collection

Twinnies. Older, smaller set from Gabriel. **$30.** Addison Collection

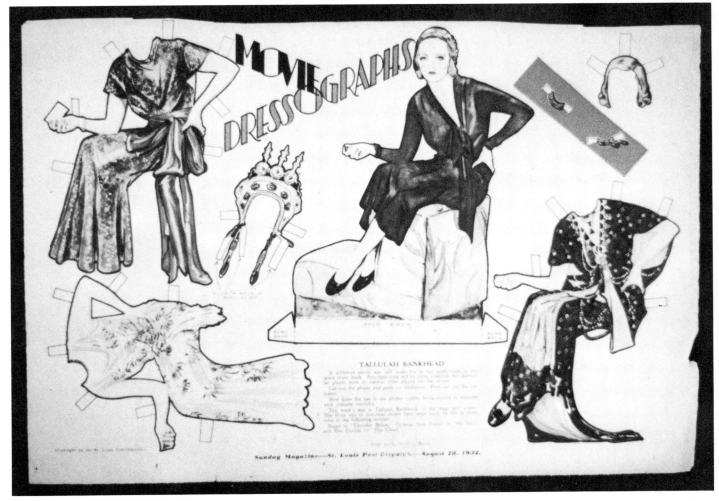

Dressograph. **$25.** Courtesy of Cynthia Musser

Hour of Charm. Saalfield #2481, 1943. **$25.** Courtesy of Rand McNally and Company

The Forties

Paper doll collectibles and nostalgia seem to center around big B's in the forties. There was the big war, the big book, the big bands, and the big stars.

In 1939 the Germans invaded Poland, and the decade of the forties began with ominous militaristic rumblings, a sound that influenced the 1940 United States elections.

Breaking American tradition, President Franklin Roosevelt ran and was elected to a third term. To the majority of voters, he was a heroic leader who had eased us out of the hard times of the Depression, and many also wished the security of known leadership in a world in peril of war. On December 7, 1941, Japan attacked Pearl Harbor and America went to war. So did paper dolls. Dolls in uniform include:

Saalfield
   321 Red, White, and Blue, 1943
   2445 Victory Paper Dolls, 1943
   2446 Army and Navy Wedding Party, 1943
   2450 Uncle Sam's Little Helpers, 1943
   2468 Stage Door Canteen, 1943

Lowe
   1048 Girls in Uniform, 1942
   1074 Tom the Aviator, 1941
   1074 Harry the Soldier, 1941
   1074 Dick the Sailor, 1941

Girls in Uniform. Lowe. **$15.** Courtesy of Samuel Lowe Company Inc.

Paper dolls went to war too. **$15.**

Victory, Saalfield: Courtesy Rand McNally and Company.
WACS and WAVES, Whitman: Reprinted by permission of Western Publishing Company, Inc.

Merrill
   3424 Victory Volunteers, 1942
   3425 Army Nurse and Doctor, 1942
   3428 Navy Scouts, 1942
   3451 Paper Doll Wedding, 1943
   3452 Girl Pilots of the Ferry Command, 1943
   3477 Liberty Belles, 1943
   3481 Soldiers and Sailors House Party, 1943

Whitman
   985 WACS and WAVES, 1943
   3980 Our Sailor Bob, 1943
   3980 Our Soldier Jim, 1943
   3980 Our WAC Joan, 1943

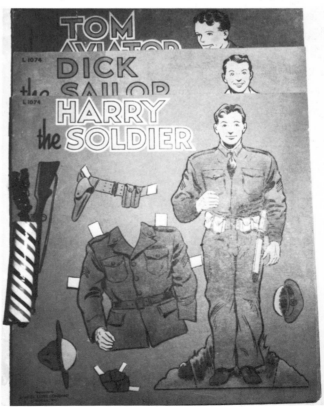

Tom Aviator, Dick Sailor, Harry Soldier. Lowe. **$18.**

Samuel Lowe Publishing Company. In 1940 Samuel Lowe left the Whitman Publishing Company to begin his own firm, the Samuel Lowe Publishing Company, in Kenosha, Wisconsin. Lowe had worked with paper dolls for Whitman for twenty-three years, and he was important to that company's success. It was Lowe's idea to begin the big-little books for Whitman that some of us remember from our childhoods. Lowe's new firm produced paper dolls immediately.

Lowe was president of the company until his death in 1952, when Edith Lowe became president. The company has used several names since 1955: James and Jonathan, John Martin's House, Abbott Publishing, Angelus Publishing, Lolly Pop Books, and Faircrest.

In 1940 rumblings of war were not all that occupied the American press. In 1936 Margaret Mitchell's *Gone with the Wind* was published and was a sensation. A million copies were sold in six months, and the 1947 sales figures topped the old best-selling record book, *Uncle Tom's Cabin.* Producer David O. Selznick and M. G. M. Studios purchased the screen rights.

Clark Gable was the obvious choice to play Rhett Butler, and they waited three years for him to be available. But the question before the nation was who would play Scarlett?

Scarlett and Rhett. Merrill, #3405.
Courtesy of Merrill Co., Publishers (Jean Woodcock). Addison Collection.

The widely publicized search for Scarlett took time, and the final decision to use an unknown English actress, Vivien Leigh, to play a Southern belle caused much consternation and head shaking in moviedom.

In fact, the filming of a book of such epic scope met with great negativism everywhere in Hollywood. Jack Warner, Olivia de

Haviland's boss, is reported to have said, "You don't want to be in that—it's going to be the turkey of all time."

The shooting began in January, 1939. The first director, George Cukor, was fired after three weeks. The second director, Victor Fleming, had a nervous collapse, and finally shared the directorship with three others, a fact that angered him so much he refused to collect his Oscar. They ran out of money, and the cast worked on three different sets eighteen hours a day. However, the movie was finished in time for its December, 1939, opening. It is still considered a great box office masterpiece.

Two Merrill paper dolls of *Gone with the Wind* were published to tie in with the movie. Like the book and the film, the paper dolls are still big box office. Collectors adore them.

The paper dolls were beautifully executed under Merrill's direction, and the costumes relate perfectly to each costume change in the film. Cut or uncut, to a collector the Gone with the Wind paper doll is a prize of epic proportion.

Gone with the Wind. Merrill, #3405, 1940. Cover artist: Frances Corett. **$100 up.** Courtesy of Merrill Co., Publishers (Jean Woodcock)

Costume pages from five-doll Gone with the Wind.

Costume page from eighteen-doll Gone with the Wind. Artists: George Trimmer, Carol Loury, Christine Chisholm, and Florence Salter. **$100 up.** Courtesy of Merrill Co., Publishers (Jean Woodcock)

Music and youth have always had a special affinity. In the forties it was the big bands and the bobby soxers jitterbugging to "Tuxedo Junction," "Chattanooga Choo Choo," and "String of Pearls." The "Hit Parade" announced the top ten songs, and the list of the big bands tootling them out is music history. Glenn Miller, Harry James, Tommy Dorsey, Gene Krupa, and Benny Goodman made the waxes, and Samuel Lowe made paper dolls of Glenn Miller and Benny Goodman.

There is not enough space in this book to illustrate all the collectible and highly sought movie star paper dolls from this period. The forties have been called the golden years of movies. In 1948 ticket sales were almost three and one-half billion dollars. America loved movies, and America loved movie stars. All paper doll collectors know that the true sign of stardom in the forties and fifties was not a footprint in front of Grauman's Chinese Theater, but rather, a paper doll book done by Merrill, Whitman, Saalfield, or Lowe. Time has turned the dolls from this era into paper doll classics. Dolls from Merrill Publishing are the most highly sought.

Movie Star Dolls of the 1940s

1940:

Whitman

156	Gloria Jean
989	Jane Withers
996	Baby Sandy (Queen Holden)
999	Judy Garland (Queen Holden)
3492	Sonja Henie

Saalfield

| 1787 | Shirley Temple |

Merrill

3404	Gone with the Wind (18 dolls)
3405	Gone with the Wind (5 Dolls)
3480	Deanna Durbin
3488	Dionne Quintuplets
3500	Let's Play House with the Dionne Quintuplets (A-Cecile, B-Annette, C-Emilie, D-Yvonne, E-Marie)

1941:

Whitman

968	Four Mothers and Their Babies (Lane sisters)
980	Judy Garland
986	Jane Withers
989	Betty Grable

Saalfield

1664	Gloria Jean
1666	Gloria Jean
2356	Charlie Chaplin and Paulette Goddard

Merrill

3418	Sonja Henie
3426	Baby Sandy
3438	Tyrone Power and Linda Darnell
3460	Jeanette MacDonald
3461	Jeanette MacDonald Costume Parade
3466	Ziegfeld Girl
4800	Alice Faye
4804	Deanna Durbin

Lowe

| 4041 | Hollywood Personalities (cast of *Holiday Inn*) |

1942:

Whitman

| 972 | Betty Grable (box) |
| 976 | Bob Hope and Dorothy Lamour |

The Dionne Quints. Merrill, #3488, 1940. **$75 up.**
Courtesy of Merrill Co., Publishers (Jean Woodcock)

The beat: Glenn Miller and Marion Hutton. Samuel Lowe.
Courtesy of Samuel Lowe Company Inc.

Charlie Chaplin. Saalfield, #2356, 1941. **$80.** Courtesy of Rand McNally and Company

Big bands: Glenn Miller and Benny Goodman. Samuel Lowe. **$80.** Courtesy of Samuel Lowe Company Inc.

Shirley Temple. Saalfield, #3425, 1942. **$40 up.** Courtesy of Rand McNally and Company

Collectors search for these Merrills: Jeanette MacDonald, **$60;** *Bette Davis,* **$60;** *Alice Faye,* **$75.** Courtesy of Merrill Co., Publishers (Jean Woodcock)

Betty Davis wardrobe. Courtesy of Merrill Co., Publishers (Jean Woodcock)

Singing star of the forties, Deanna Durbin, Merrill #3480, 1940, **$60 and up.** *#4804, 1941,* **$70 and up.**
Courtesy of Merrill Co., Publishers (Jean Woodcock)

984	Carolyn Lee
988	Lana Turner
991	Movie Starlets
995	Carmen Miranda
1016	Betty Brewer
1016	Cora Sue Collins
1016	Virginia Weidler

Saalfield

1539	Mary Martin
2425	Shirley Temple
2426	Joan Carrol

Merrill

3478	Rita Hayworth
3482	Hedy Lamarr
4816	Bette Davis

1945:

Whitman

975	Lana Turner
996	Judy Garland

Saalfield

2503	Claudette Colbert

1946:

Whitman

960	Movie Starlets
963	Margaret O'Brien
964	Margaret O'Brien
976	Betty Grable

1947:

Whitman

964	Lana Turner
992	Gene Tierney

1948:

Whitman

995	Roy Rogers

Saalfield

1529	Rita Hayworth

1949:

Whitman

165	Ava Gardner
968	Elizabeth Taylor

Hollywood Personalities. Stars of the movie Holiday Inn. *Samuel Lowe, #1049, 1941.* **$70 up.**
Courtesy of Samuel Lowe Company Inc.

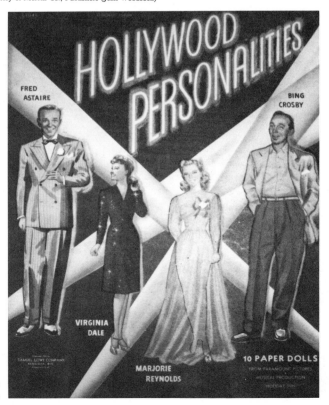

Stars of the movie Ziegfield Follies: *Hedy Lamarr, Judy Garland, and Lana Turner. Merrill, 1941.* **$75 up.**

Courtesy of Merrill Co., Publishers (Jean Woodcock). Addison Collection

Rita Hayworth as Carmen. Saalfield, #2712, 1948. **$25.**   Courtesy of Rand McNally and Company

The Fifties

The fifties have passed just long enough now to seem nostalgic. Despite the cold war, the Korean War, and McCarthyism, the postwar years of presidents Truman and Eisenhower, years of the baby and the building boom, seem today to emit an aura of happiness.

McCall's, a family magazine, created the togetherness credo for family life. Helped by low down payments and G. I. Loans, families moved to the suburbs in masses. They built thousands of dreamhouses, ranches with picture windows, patios, and T. V. antennas.

These were the days of *The Organization Man, The Man in the Gray Flannel Suit,* the Barbie doll, T. V., Mouseketeers, 3-D glasses, Cinerama, Cinemascope, the hoola hoop, Elvis Presley, and rock and roll. The Russians launched Sputnik. Uneeda Doll launched Wishnik. Whitman made the paper doll. Queen Elizabeth was crowned, and a paper doll commemorated the event.

The fifties were peak paper doll production years. They were the last years of the movie star paper dolls and the first years of the T. V. star paper doll. It is a wonderful era for collectors.

Most notable fifties collectible dolls, of course, are the Merrill Company's Betty Grable, Esther Williams, and Hedy Lamarr; the Saalfield's Marilyn Monroe, and the Whitman's Grace Kelly. Most representative of the period paper doll are the many sets of Elizabeth Taylor, Debbie Reynolds, Doris Day, and June Allyson.

The most interesting background story of the fifties paper dolls comes from the file of the Saalfield Marilyn Monroe paper doll. It was a problem doll. It was late. Paper dolls were sold to the chains in advance of their publication. Everyone looked forward to the Monroe doll, and it had not come off the presses.

Movie star paper dolls were negotiated at their inception through agents and studios, and the stars retained the right to approve the artistic renderings of the book before publication. For most books, this was a routine procedure. But Marilyn Monroe discussed her paper doll with the studio art department, and together they concluded that the paper dolls were not sexy enough. They would have to be redrawn.

The fifties have an aura of happiness. Paper dolls from Samuel Lowe: Junior Misses, $6; *Prom,* $10.
Courtesy of Samuel Lowe Company Inc.

Hanging out 1950s. Lowe junior miss paper doll. Courtesy of Samuel Lowe Company Inc.

The coronation paper dolls and coloring book. Saalfield, #4312, 1953. **$20.** Courtesy of Rand McNally and Company

Elizabeth crowned queen.

From the Hollywood representative apologizing for the delays came this in November, 1952:

> She made the changes personally with the aid of the studio art department and must be followed to the letter. . . . Sorry, no control. . . . She is the one star that is being groomed and exploited and guarded so carefully. She is the only one we will run into this kind of trouble with.

The paper doll came out in 1954. It was well worth waiting for!

On April 18, 1956, the beautiful actress Grace Kelly married Prince Albert Ranier of Monaco in the biggest wedding of the century. The marriage was enormous fifties news, and the story adds fairytale luster to already lovely sets of paper dolls, making them exceptionally collectible. This is from Whitman.

Betty Grable. Merrill, #1558, 1951. **$40.**
Courtesy of Merrill Co., Publishers (Jean Woodcock)

Elizabeth Taylor. Whitman, #973 (left) 1950, **$40;**
#1951 (right) 1955, **$30.**
Courtesy of Elizabeth Taylor. Reprinted by permission of Western Publishing Company, Inc.

Esther Williams. Merrill, #1563, 1950. **$40.**
Courtesy of Merrill Co., Publishers (Jean Woodcock)

The Saalfield files in the Kent State Library contain this indignant letter to the Saalfield editor from the artist's representative in response to Monroe's changes:

> Miss Monroe says about that coat ''bad neckline—lower—give a bust line—make all outfits look sexier—colors are good.'' One does not wear plunging neckline red coats, not even when one is Miss Monroe. So I should like to ignore that suggestion. . . . She says about the black nightgown ''more sheer and better shaped.'' Now really, are you going to sell this under the counter or in Paris as postcards? . . . But we'll do a little about this to make it more acceptable to her and yet not have you in the courts for corrupting the morals of our young.

Movie Star Dolls of the 1950s

1950:
  Whitman
    970   June Allyson
  Merrill
   1563   Esther Williams
1951:
  Whitman
   1185   Jane Powell

Saalfield
  2600   Hedy Lamarr
Merrill
  1558   Betty Grable

1952:
Whitman
  1171   Jane Powell
  1193   Elizabeth Taylor
  2103   Doris Day
Saalfield
  1557   Faye Emerson
  1558   Carmen Miranda

1953:
Whitman
  1171   Jane Powell
  1173   June Allyson
  1177   Elizabeth Taylor
  2108   Ava Gardner
Dell
  Debbie Reynolds
Saalfield
  1584   Linda Darnell
  1587   Arlene Dahl
  2725   Joan Caulfield
  2731   Laraine Day
  4311   Arlene Dahl
Merrill
  2551   Piper Laurie
  2552   Betty Grable
  2553   Esther Williams Cut Outs and Color
  2554   Janet Leigh

1954:
Whitman
  1954   Doris Day
  2112   Elizabeth Taylor
Saalfield
  1591   Judy Holliday
  4318   Barbara Britton
  4323   Marilyn Monroe
  5190   Barbara Britton
  5191   Rhonda Fleming

1955:
Whitman
  1951   Elizabeth Taylor
  1952   Doris Day
  1955   Debbie Reynolds
  1956   June Allyson
  2049   Grace Kelly
  2055   Jane Powell
Saalfield
  2611   Diana Lynn
  2651   Jane Russell
Dell
  Pier Angeli

Stylish wardrobe of Elizabeth Taylor. Whitman, 1950.
Courtesy of Elizabeth Taylor. Reprinted by permission of Western Publishing Company, Inc.

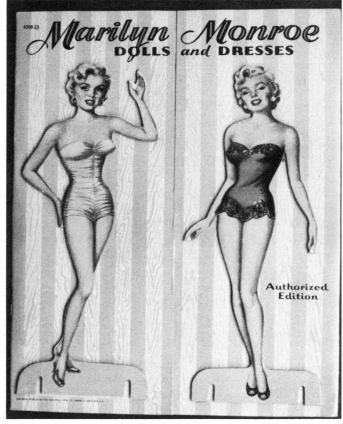

Marilyn Monroe. Saalfield, #4308, 1953. $60 up.
Courtesy of Rand McNally and Company

Coat of Miss Monroe.

Debbie Reynolds, Whitman, 1955. **$30.**
Courtesy of Debbie Reynolds. Reprinted by permission of Western Publishing, Inc.

Doris Day. Whitman, 1952. **$30.**
Courtesy of Doris Day. Reprinted by permission of Western Publishing Company, Inc.

Grace Kelly. Whitman, #2049, 1955. **$50.**
Courtesy of H. S. H. Princess Grace of Monaco. Reprinted by permission of Western Publishing Company, Inc.

1956:
  Whitman
    1952   Doris Day
    2084   Cyd Charisse
    2609   Grace Kelly
1957:
  Whitman
    1955   Debbie Reynolds
    1962   Natalie Wood
    1977   Doris Day
    2057   Elizabeth Taylor
    2068   Vera Miles

2085	Jane Powell
2087	Rock Hudson
2089	June Allyson

Saalfield

4409	Kim Novak
4422	Virginia Mayo
4442	Sheree North

1958:

Whitman

| 2086 | Natalie Wood |

Dell

Debra Paget

Saalfield

4423	Martha Hyer
4429	Kim Novak
4441	Joanne Woodward
4474	Julie Andrews
6032	Shirley Temple Play Kit

1959:

Whitman

| 1966 | Marge and Gower Champion |
| 4413 | Sandra Dee |

Saalfield

| 4420 | Shirley Temple |

Television began in 1946 with the National Broadcasting Company's telecast of a Joe Louis and Billy Conn fight. Broadcasts of Congress, baseball, Howdy Doody, and Kukla, Fran, and Ollie followed. For a time, most of the country watched static, but New York and Los Angeles had seven stations.

As television grew, its effects were enormous. Sid Caesar and Imogene Coca kept watchers home on Saturday nights. In 1951 there was a 20 to 40 percent drop in movie attendance, depending on location. Mass entertainment began to be spelled T. V.! Naturally, child-oriented, family television programs were mirrored in the paper doll.

Television Dolls of the 1950s

1950:

Whitman

990	Gene Autry's Melody Ranch
998	Roy Rogers and Dale Evans
1186	Roy Rogers and Dale Evans

1951:

Whitman

| 1184 | Gene Autry at Melody Ranch |

1952:

Whitman

| 1172 | Roy Rogers and Dale Evans |
| 2104 | Mary Hartline |

1953:

Whitman

1175	Mary Hartline
2101	Lucille Ball and Desi Arnaz
2116	Lucille Ball, Desi Arnaz, and Little Ricky
2118	Roy Rogers and Dale Evans

Saalfield

| 1585 | Eve Arden |
| 4310 | Eve Arden |

1954:

Whitman

1950	Roy Rogers and Dale Evans
2042	Dinah Shore
2737	My Little Margie

1955:

Whitman

| 2044 | Mary Hartline |

1956:

Whitman

1950	Roy Rogers and Dale Evans
1958	Annette (Funicello, Mouseketeer)
2060	Dinah Shore
2083	Annette

E. Lowe

| 2560 | The Honeymooners |

Saalfield

| 2746 | Eve Arden |
| 4352 | Loretta Young |

1957:

Whitman

1950	Roy Rogers, Dale Evans, and Dusty
1974	Mouseketeers
1979	Lennon Sisters

Saalfield

1727	The Story Princess (Arlene Dalton)
2759	Spanky and Darla
4421	Gisele MacKenzie

Dell

| 117 | Gale Storm |

1958:

Whitman

1957	Linda (Hughes, Mouseketeer)
1958	Darlene
1963	Dinah Shore
1964	Janet Lennon
1979	Lennon Sisters
2061	Gale Storm

Samuel Lowe

| 2732 | The Bob Cummins Fashion Models |

Saalfield

4442	Polly Bergen
4447	Shari Lewis
4475	Gisele MacKenzie

1959:

Whitman

1938	McGuire Sisters
1943	Captain Kangaroo (punchout)
1956	Janet Lennon
1959	Edd ''Kookie'' Byrnes
1968	Pat Boone
1970	Dinah Shore and George Montgomery
1991	Lennon Sisters
2089	Gale Storm

Saalfield

| 4415 | Anne Sothern |

Roy Rogers and Dale Evans. Whitman. **$20.**

Courtesy of Roy Rogers Enterprises, Inc. Reprinted by permission of Western Publishing Company, Inc.

The Sixties

If the fifties were "togetherness" years, the sixties were the antithesis, for through protest, riot, racism, drugs, violence, rebellion, and war, American society came "unglued."

"Togetherness" slipped happily enough into the beginning years of the decade, however, with the election of John F. Kennedy and his idealistic New Frontier platform. At forty-six, Kennedy was our youngest elected president, and he and his cultivated, beautiful, socialite wife Jacqueline brought elegance and style to Washington.

Three paper dolls of the Kennedys were published by Magic Wand Publishing. As America's first family, the Kennedys seemed to many to be magically charismatic. Sadly, John Kennedy's presidential term was brief. He was assassinated in Dallas, Texas, on November 22, 1963. Writers have dubbed the Kennedy White House America's Camelot, and none of the popular news clairvoyants could possibly have predicted at decade's beginning the sequence of events that turned First Lady Jacqueline Kennedy into Mrs. Aristotle Onassis.

Paper dolls of the sixties, I believe, will become highly sought collectibles and *now* is the time to find them, as these are the dolls that are currently emerging inexpensively in garage sales and flea markets.

It was a far-out decade, beginning with Kennedy paper dolls and ending with Nixon. Historically, it will be remembered for important scientific advances from the heart transplant to the Pill to the conquest of space.

On April 12, 1961, Russian Cosmonaut Yuri Gagarin orbited earth, followed twenty-three days later by U. S. Astronaut Alan B. Shepard, Jr.

In mid-decade, July, 1975, the East and the West, in the form of U. S. Spacecraft Apollo and Soviet Spacecraft Soyez, docked in space above Amsterdam, and U. S. Commodore Thomas Stafford shook the hand of his Russian counterpart, Alexei Leonov.

On July 12, 1969, American Apollo Moon Mission pilots Neil Armstrong and Edwin Aldrin successfully separated their spacecraft from the Apollo II, piloted by Michael Collins. The enthralled world watched the televised event and heard Armstrong say, "The Eagle has wings," and later, "The Eagle has landed. Tranquility Base here."

Man had reached the moon! Six and one-half hours later, Armstrong, in a proud moment for the U. S., descended the Eagle's ladder, touching the lunar surface and sending back to earth the words, "That's one small step for man, one giant leap for mankind."

The achievement of space was not, as such, made into a paper doll. However, Major Matt Mason, a 1969 Whitman version of the popular toy space figure made by Mattel, does reflect the country's enthusiasm for the space effort. This pressout book includes wonderful space gear and a lunar landscape. A sixties collection should surely contain a book that includes the moon.

The sixties were the decade of culture and counterculture, of race riots and peace demonstrations, of youth rebelling against the draft, Vietnam, the establishment, government, and technology. Colorful words spelled it out. There were hippies, yippies, flower power, communes, Freedom Riders, sit-ins, happenings, fuzz, S. D. S., Weathermen, and pot. There were places like Alice's Restaurant, Berkeley, Watts, Woodstock, and Carnaby Street.

Paper dolls represented the establishment. However, counterculture and youth influenced the establishment in this period,

Jackie Kennedy giant 31" paper doll. Magic Wand. **$25.**

John-John Kennedy paper doll. Magic Wand. **$20.**

especially in the "threads" and groovy fashions worn by all paper dolls and presented in the art style of the period, psychedelic. In waves of vivid color and zippy symbols, miniskirts, midis, hot pants, boots, tights, hippie fringes, Granny ponchos, big bells, Indian necklaces, and guru beads all rock on paper doll pages.

Mod style was exported from England in the sixties. Mary Quant was the originator, and Carnaby Street was the London location. There, little specialty shops known as boutiques sprang up to cater to the swinging tastes of the young. Twiggy, English model Leslie Hornsby, was the epitome of Mod. She was charming, tiny, skinny, photogenic with big eyes, and a flapperish bob. In her short miniskirts, she captured for both America and England the approved essence of the sixties. Whitman made a wonderfully collectible paper doll of her in 1967.

In the 1950s Elvis Presley was king of rock and roll. In 1963 the British Beatles took rock in a new direction. With the hit, "I Want to Hold Your Hand," the Liverpool group, composed of John Lennon, Paul McCartney, George Harrison, and Ringo Starr, began the "Beatlemania" that caused teeny-bopper riots on both sides of the Atlantic and made all the singers millionaires.

After making movies like *A Hard Day's Night, Help,* and *Let It Be;* composing and performing classic rock music; and establishing their own recording company, Apple Records, the group disbanded in 1971. Whitman did a paper pressout mobile of the group in 1964, which should be a part of any representative sixties paper doll collection.

Inspired by the English Beatles, Columbia Pictures in 1966 decided to do a television series based on a rock group. After an extensive search Michael Nesmith, Mickey Dolenz, Peter Tork, and Davy Jones were organized as the Monkees. They, too, were a teeny-bopper success, and Whitman made the punchout book in 1966.

Paper doll lore states that a prominent editor of a prominent paper doll publisher said in the sixties, "Paper dolls are dead." Little girls no longer seemed to play avidly with paper dolls. However, there was not a fourth-grade counterculture movement. Every child was too busy playing Barbie and Ken to bother with cutting out paper dolls. (See Barbie and Betsy chapter.)

Nevertheless, there were some diehard paper dolls produced, and kid-vid television programs were turned into paper dolls that are most collectible today. Most popular were the "Mouseketeers." Young and old could hum the theme, and black beanies with mouse ears were big sellers. Paper dolls were made of the group, and numerous books were made of Annette Funicello, the program's most popular star.

Nothing could diminish the appeal of Walt Disney creations, and the decade that produced *Hair* also produced enchanting family charmers like *Mary Poppins,* a musical. Julie Andrews and Dick Van Dyke appeared in the movie. Whitman made two books of Mary Poppins. Disney also produced the movies *Summer Magic, That Darn Cat,* and *The Happiest Millionaire,* all of which turned paper doll. *My Fair Lady* was another lovely stage and movie production of the 1960s. Two paper dolls were made of this.

118

The decade ended with Nixon paper dolls. Artcraft. **$12.**
Courtesy of Rand McNally and Company

Sixties fashion, Nixon style. Courtesy of Rand McNally and Company

Major Matt Mason. Whitman, 1969. Doll of Mattel space figure reflected space enthusiasm. **$6.**
Reprinted by permission of Western Publishing Company, Inc.
©1972, Mattel, Inc. Trademarks of Mattel, Inc. used with permission.

Twiggy was the perfect Mod model. Reprinted by permission of Western Publishing Company, Inc.

Psychedelic graphics from Whitman. (Reprints still on the market.) Reprinted by permission of Western Publishing Company, Inc.

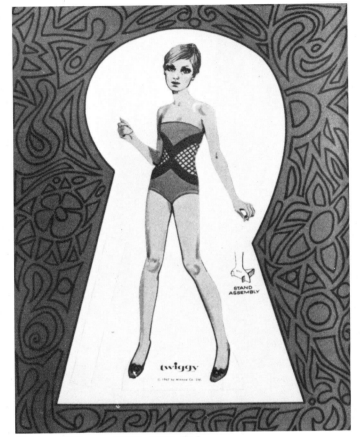

Twiggy. Whitman, #2809, 1962. **$15.**

Twiggy "threads."

Television Dolls of the 1960s

1960:
Whitman
- 1971   Annette
- 1991   Dennis the Menace (Jay North)
- 1996   Dennis the Menace
- 4718   Lennon Sisters (box)

1961:
Whitman
- 1948   Janet Lennon
- 1958   National Velvet (Lori Martin)
- 1961   Annette in Hawaii
- 1983   Lennon Sisters
- 4614   Connie Stevens ("Hawaiian Eye")

Saalfield
- 2743   Donna Reed

1962:
Whitman
- 1956   Annette
- 2089   Ginny Tai
- 2091   Molly Bee
- 4613   Janet Lennon
- 4621   Annette
- 4798   Lennon Sisters (box)

Lowe
- 2740   Dr. Kildare (Richard Chamberlain)

Saalfield
- 6043   Shari Lewis and Her Puppets

1963:
Whitman
- 1964   Patty Duke
- 1965   Patty Duke
- 1974   Mouseketeers
- 1975   The Nurses
- 1991   Lucy and Her TV Family
- 4610   Lucy

Watkins/Strathmore
- 1819A   Elly May
- 1919A   Cynthia Pepper ("Margie")

Milton Bradley
- 1963   Patty Duke

1964:
Whitman
- 1949   Beverly Hillbillies
- 1953   Annette
- 1954   Petticoat Junction
- 1955   Beverly Hillbillies
- 1963   Lucy

Saalfield
- 4440   Hootenanny

Merry
- 6403   Donna Reed

1965:
Magic Wand
- Bewitched

Saalfield
- Karen ("90 Bristol Court")

1966:
Whitman
- 1926   Lassie
- 1959   The Munsters

Magic Wand
- 115   Tabitha ("Bewitched")

1967:
Whitman
- 1979   Green Acres

Saalfield
- 6066   That Girl

1968:
Whitman
- 1965   Buffy
- 4667   Family Affair
- 4773   Green Acres

Saalfield
- 4434   Blondie
- 5131   Flying Nun
- 6055   Julia

Colorforms
- 355   Julia

1969:
Saalfield
- 1325   Laugh-In

Movie Star Dolls of the 1960s

1960:
Whitman
- 1956   Debbie Reynolds
- 2089   Mary Poppins
- 5112   Tuesday Weld

Golden Press
- 67163   Hayley Mills *(Pollyanna)*

1961:
Whitman
- 715   Hayley Mills *(Summer Magic)*

1962:
Whitman
- 1948   Debbie Reynolds

1963:
Whitman
- 1966   Hayley Mills *(Summer Magic)*

1964:
Whitman
- 1982   Mary Poppins

1965:
Whitman
- 1955   Hayley Mills *(That Darn Cat)*

Ottenheimer
- 2960   My Fair Lady
- 5860   My Fair Lady

1967:
Saalfield
- 4487   Happiest Millionaire

1968:
Saalfield
- 1336   Finian's Rainbow

The era of Hair *also produced family shows like the movie* Mary Poppins *and kid-vid like "Mouseketeers."*

Paper doll books. Whitman. **$8.**

The Seventies

The early seventies were an extension of the sixties. There were bombings, rallies, marches, protests, and demonstrations. Fighting in Vietnam led to the bombing of Cambodia. Nixon was president.

Most notable for paper doll collectors was the 1970 attempt of the fashion arbiters to lure the stylish woman to the French midi, the "longuette."

Women's Wear Daily and its editor, John Fairchild, considered a spokesman for couture, backed the new skirt length and the stores stocked it. The style was a fashion disaster. It became obvious that the sixties' spirit of rebellion had infiltrated Ms. Establishment. Females were no longer slaves of style and skirt lengths. Designer Ives St. Laurent gracefully capitulated, admitting that "length is no longer important. What is wonderful is the freedom to choose one's clothes."

A wonderful tongue-in-cheek satire depicted First Lady Patricia Nixon and her daughers, Tricia and Julie, on a spring shopping trip:

Once upon a time—in fact, this very spring—the wife of the President of the United States and her two fair daughters set out for New York City to buy new dresses. Now, the people all knew that the wife of the President of France was wearing her dresses long that year, and they could not wait to see if their own First Lady would follow suit.*

In a women's history illustrated by paper dolls, this would have to be step number three—women freed from the dictates of fashion.

By 1970 filmdom was completely changed from earlier. The great glamorous movie studios had disappeared, along with the movie queens. Large financial groups and conglomerates had taken over the industry. An indication of this was the auction at M. G. M. Studios of all the old costumes, scenery, and properties. Paper dolls continued to portray popular family-oriented television shows and teenage stars, but fewer were produced.

*LIFE Magazine,© 1970 Time Inc. Reprinted with permission.

Three Little Nixons. **$8.** LIFE Magazine © 1970 Time Inc. Reprinted with permission. Courtesy of John Alcorn, artist.

Television Dolls of the 1970s

1970:
Whitman
Buffy and Jody
Saalfield/Artcraft
5114 Nanny and the Professor
6055 Julia

1971:
Artcraft
4343 Curiosity Shop
5115 Dodie
5139 Hee Haw
5140 Julia
Whitman
4787 Brady Bunch
5137 Partridge Family

1972:
Colorforms
587 David Cassidy

1973:
Artcraft
5225 Marie Osmond
Estelle Ansley Worrell
Dottie West

1975:
Whitman
1995 The Waltons

1976:
Toy Factory
105 Happy Days—Fonzie (Henry Winkler, box)
106 Welcome Back Kotter—Kotter (Gabe Kaplan, box)
Whitman
1986 Shirley Temple

1977:
Toy Factory
107 Welcome Back Kotter—Barbarino (John Travolta, box)
110 Charlie's Angels—Jill (Farah Fawcett, box)
111 Charlie's Angels—Sabrina (Kate Jackson, box)
112 Charlie's Angels—Kelly (Jaclyn Smith, box)
Whitman
1991 Donny and Marie

1978:
Toy Factory
Charlie's Angels—Kris (Cheryl Ladd)

1979:
Avon
75127 Gilda Radner

Popular television: Julia.
Artcraft, #4472, $3.50.
Nanny and the Professor.
Artcraft, #4114, $3.50.

Julia courtesy of Rand McNally and Company. Nanny and the Professor courtesy of Rand McNally and Company and of Twentieth Century Fox.

For whatever reasons—the baby-boom turned twenty, stagflation economics necessitating black and white printing, decor and framability, magic markers and felt-tipped pens, contemporary wit, cleverness, fun, and madness—the adult-child coloring book paper doll, sold in book and gift stores, appeared in the early seventies and caught on.

As early as 1961, *The Executive Coloring Book,* a satire on the company president in gray flannel suit was an adult best-seller; and sophisticated, humorous, educational, and beautiful adult-child coloring books began appearing. In the early seventies the coloring books branched into sophisticated, humorous, educational, and beautiful adult-child paper dolls to color. They included:

Fashion Kit, Troubador Press, 1971 (ballet paper dolls)
Dressing Up History, Potpourri Press, 1971
Henry VIII, Bellerophon, 1972
Queen Elizabeth I, Bellerophon, 1973
Great Women Paper Dolls, Bellerophon, 1974
Infamous Women, Bellerophon, 1976

These books are still available and are an exciting new direction for paper dolls—proof that paper dolls will *never* die! From my favorite of these, Bellerophon's *Great Women,* comes the final heroine of our paper doll women's history, Golda Meir, who stated, "When my colleagues, men, look at me. . . . I say 'Don't worry. We will see to it, we women, that you have the right to vote and equal pay for equal work. And once in a while, we will even elect a man as Prime Minister!'"

In 1973, Nixon visited China, was reelected president, and committed the actions that came to be called Watergate. In 1974, peace talks began in Vietnam, and the Watergate problem erupted. On August 8, 1974, Nixon resigned. On August 9, 1974, Gerald Ford became president. On September 8, 1974, Gerald Ford granted Richard Nixon a pardon. By 1975, there were still economic and energy worries, but tension was eased in the country. News of rioters turned into news of streakers; psychedelic turned patchwork.

The Bicentennial stimulated an interest in our Colonial history, and to celebrate the nation's two-hundredth birthday,

Sesame Street. Still on the market. Incorporates fabulous graphics into paper doll. Whitman.

Adult-child coloring book paper dolls by Bellerophon. Currently on the market. Courtesy of Bellerophon Books.

fire hydrants were painted red, white, and blue; covered wagons crossed the land; and on the Fourth of July, 225 tall ships from 30 nations, led by the U. S. Eagle, sailed up the Hudson River. Bicentennial paper dolls were published by Whitman and Artcraft.

There have always been collectors. Members of every society have always tried to preserve relics from other centuries. There are many reasons for this, among them economics, sentiment, nostalgia, historic preservation, media, and knowledge. However, contemporary "collectivitis" seems at fever pitch. Beginning in the sixties, growing in the seventies and even now, almost everyone seems to have at least a touch of the fever. From beer cans, brothel tokens, china plates, metal plaques, trading cards, comic books, antique furniture, toys, dolls, stamps, coins, spoons, mugs to bells, almost everything is collected and claims at least one organized collectors' group, society, or newsletter. Paper dolls share in this enthusiasm, and as a result, some wonderful, collectible paper dolls are emerging for the collectors' market as well as the children's market. Publishers are presenting reproductions of old, imaginative adult-child paper dolls. In the seventies, Dover Publishing, Merrimac Publishing Corporation, and Evergreen Press were in the forefront.

Merrimac: Reproductions and Originals. Merrimac does not identify their originals, but labels them "replicas of the original antique." We have identified the following where

known:

Our Dollies and How to Dress Them (McLoughlin set, boxed, 1920)

Dolls of All Nations (McLoughlin, Wide World Costume Dolls)

Dilly Dollies Paper Cut-Out Dolls and Costumes (Betty Bonnet, Sheila Young, *Ladies' Home Journal,* 1915–1918)

Antique Teddy Bear (Selchow and Richter)

Antique Paper Cutout Dolls and Clothes—Exact Replica of Museum Collection of the Late 1800s (German set, House of Hapsburg)

Folk Doll Paper Cut-Out (Polly's Paper Playmates, 1910)

Jointed Lady (Littauer and Bauer, 1890s)

Kate Greenaway Antique Embossed (Original paper dolls done in manner of Kate Greenaway from illustrations. Greenaway did not draw paper dolls.)

Evergreen Press. Exquisite original paper dolls handsomely printed include:

Peggy Jo Rosamond: The Antique Dolls Go To A Paper Doll Wedding, Antique French Paper Dolls

Janet Nason (Collector's Art Series): Dolls of the 1930s Paper Dolls, Antique German Bisque Paper Dolls

Dover Publishing. The beautiful, full color, heavy stock reproduction, and exciting well-documented educational paper dolls published in the seventies include:

Golda Meir, from Great Women Paper Dolls.   Courtesy of Bellerophon Books.

Rock Flowers. Wonderful psychedelic feel. From Rosemary, Lilac, and Heather dolls by Mattel. **$3.**

Antique Paper Dolls of the Edwardian Era

Antique Paper Dolls 1915–1920 (Arnold Arnold)

Victorian Fashion Paper Dolls from *Harper's Bazaar*
(Theodore Menton's lovely creations from *Harper's* fashion plates)

Fashion Paper Dolls From *Godey's Lady's Book* (Susan Johnson's lovely creations from *Godey's* fashion plates)

Dolly Dingle (Grace G. Drayton)

Glamorous Movie Stars of the Thirties (Original, Tom Tierney)

Erte Fashion Paper Dolls of the Twenties (Susan Johnson's stunning creations from original Erte drawings)

Antique Jumping Jacks (Pantins from Epinal)

Rudolph Valentino (Original, Tom Tierney)

Marilyn Monroe Paper Dolls (Original, Tom Tierney)

Independent Artists. One wishes there were space in this volume to illustrate the exciting paper dolls that independent artists are currently printing. Their work can be purchased from the paper dolls sources listed in Appendix E. They are occasionally advertised in paper doll newsletters. A sampling of independent artists whose paper dolls are sought and cherished by collectors are: Marilyn Henry, Helen Page, Richard Rusnock, Lou Valentino, Pat Stall, Margie Bergener, Ernest Rumbarger, Gordon Anderson, Emma Terry, Susan Sirkus, and Bruce Patrick Jones.

Casual Co. *Art Deco Whitman book, #1987, 1972.* **$2.**

Bicentennial paper dolls: Paper dolls of Early America (still on market); Colonial America. Artcraft. **$1.**

Paper Dolls of Early America reprinted by permission of Western Publishing Company, Inc.
Colonial America courtesy of Rand McNally and Co.

Country mood takes the place of groovy. Whitman (currently on the market). Reprinted by permission of Western Publishing Company, Inc.

Psychedelic turned patchwork. From Paper Dolls of Early America.

Reprinted by permission of Western Publishing Company, Inc.

Collectible poster from Des Moines Sunday Register. *1976 Ford-Carter election.* **$2.** Courtesy of the *Des Moines Sunday Register*

A trio of collectible Dover paper dolls by Tom Tierney: Pavlova and Nijinsky Paper Dolls; Marilyn Monroe Paper Dolls; Rudolph Valentino Paper Dolls. (Currently on the market, see Appendix E.)

Amy. Magic Wand. **$4.**

"It's affordable. Is it collectible?"

Courtesy Chronicle Features, San Francisco. William Hamilton, artist.

Betsy and Barbie. A 1950 Betsy McCall and a 1980 Barbie at a campsite at Lucky Lake.

McCall's Publishing Company. Reprinted by permission of Western Publishing Company, Inc.©1980, Mattel, Inc. Trademarks of Mattel, Inc. used with permission.

Betsy and Barbie

Betsy and Barbie had to be saved for last. This stalwart, stylish pair has trendily survived some of the most fascinating and tumultuous years of American history. They are most interesting paper dolls, and *now* is the time to collect them. The price is right. Their condition is mint.

Betsy. Betsy McCall is the elder. She first appeared in *McCall's Magazine* in May, 1951, appearing monthly through 1966, and almost monthly from 1967 to 1974. Thereafter, sadly, she has appeared sporadically. Numerous artists have drawn Betsy (as illustrated), and her appearance has changed over the years. Nevertheless, as *McCall's* stated when asked Betsy's age, ''She's just as old as the child who asks.''

From Betsy's inception, sturdily-printed cards with Betsy's family and friends have been available from *McCall's,* and these, too, have changed and are collectible. There have been other variations. Whitman Publishing has produced Betsy. Gabriel published a large, three-dimensional Betsy, and Simon and Schuster published a Betsy McCall story. All are collectible.

Barbie. From Mattel comes this information:

> The Barbie doll was created as a result of Ruth Handler . . . observing her own daughter playing with paper dolls. Ruth Handler observed that her daughter enjoyed paper doll play, but was interested only in those paper dolls of adult figures. It became apparent to Ruth Handler that her daughter could have more fun with a ''three-dimensional'' doll that would have a variety of miniature outfits to wear, just like the paper dolls.
>
> Ruth Handler's intuition was correct, and, as a result, the Barbie doll in 1958 became the first adult figure doll introduced in the American marketplace.

The Barbie doll became, of course, a phenomenon that introduced a new adult plastic doll era. She is still found in multivarieties with friends and buddies in today's toy stores. Since Barbie was responsible, in great part, for the 1960s lack of interest in paper dolls and therefore a lessening of paper doll production, most paper doll collectors have viewed her with mixed feelings. However, the Barbie doll is, in turn, the Barbie paper doll, and one must admit that, over the years, a parade of Barbies makes a most fascinating collection.

Whitman Publishing introduced the Barbie paper doll in 1962. Her face and hair have changed with the times, as have her graphics. In the company of her little sisters Skipper and Tutti, her faithful boyfriend Ken, and her friends Midge, Francie, Casey, Stacey, P. J., Brad, Kelly, Starr, and Shawn, one must acknowledge that Barbie is a contemporary paper perspective all by herself.

Barbie Dolls

Whitman, unless specified otherwise.

1962:
- 1962 Barbie
- 1963 Barbie and Ken
- 1971 Barbie and Ken
- 4601 Barbie
- 4797 Barbie and Ken Suitcase (box)

1963:
- 1962 Barbie
- 1962 Midge, Barbie's Best Friend
- 1976 Barbie and Ken
- 1976 Barbie, Ken, and Midge
- 4601 Barbie (box)
- 4797 Barbie and Ken
- 11001 Barbie

1964:
- 1944 Barbie and Skipper
- 1957 Barbie and Skipper
- 4605 Barbie
- 4605 Barbie, Wedding Dress 'n Fashion Clothes
- 4607 Skipper's Day-by-Day Wardrobe
- 4616 Barbie's Travel Wardrobe (box)
- 1976-59 Barbie Costume Dolls (Skipper, Ken, Midge, and Allan)

1965:
- 1984 Skipper, Barbie's Little Sister
- 1985 Skooter, Skipper's Friend
- 4605 Barbie Fashion Window Wardrobe
- 4639 Skooter Fashion Go-Round (box)
- 4778 Skipper and Skooter, Four Seasons Wardrobe
- 4785 Travel Wardrobe (box)
- 4793 Barbie, Midge, and Skipper (box)

GROWING UP WITH BETSY McCALL

1951   1956   1960   1963

It was way back in May of 1951 when Betsy first appeared in our pages. She was five going on six, and she lived in a little white house with her mother and father and a dachshund named Nosy. Over the years Betsy has grown a little older, acquired a twin brother and sister named Kerry and Merry, and gotten herself involved in all manner of things, from UNICEF to the Girl Scouts. She has received thousands of letters—some from mothers who remember Betsy when they were children—and the most-asked question is: How old is Betsy McCall? And the answer: Just as old as the child who asks.

1966   1968   1971   1976

Since May, 1951, the face and figure of Betsy has changed. McCall's, *April, 1976.*
Permission McCall's Publishing Company.

Over the years Betsy has been involved and active in community service. **$2.50.** Permission McCall's Publishing Company.

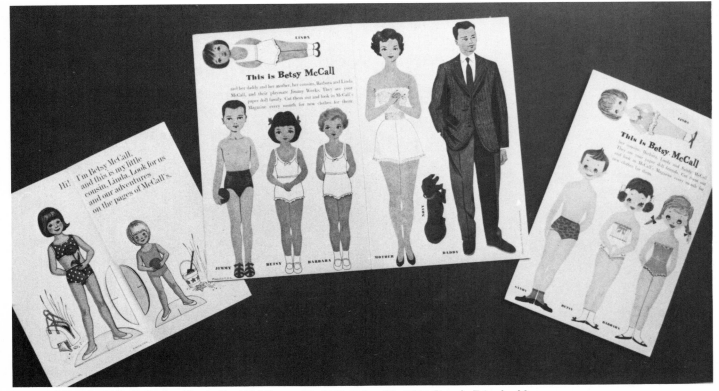

Betsy and Her Card Family (ordered by mail): 1980 Betsy, **$1;** *1951 Betsy,* **$2;** *1955 Betsy's Friends,* **$2.** Permission McCall's Publishing Company.

1966:

  1976 Barbie, Skipper, and Skooter
  1980 Meet Francie, Barbie's Modern Cousin
  4793 Barbie and Francie, Barbie's Modern Cousin (box)

1967:

  1094 Francie
  1976 Barbie Has a New Look
  1989 Francie, Barbie's Modern Cousin, and Casey,
         Francie's Fun Friend
  4622 Tutti (box)
  4701 Barbie Paper Dolls (box)
  4785 Barbie

1968:

  1976 Barbie, Christie, and Stacey, Barbie's New Friends
  1978 Barbie, Christie, and Stacey
  1991 Tutti, Barbie, and Skipper's Tiny Sister

Varieties of Betsy. Betsy McCall Biggest Paper Doll. Gabriel. **$18;**
Betsy McCall's Paper Doll Story Book. Simon and Schuster, 1954. **$18;**
Betsy McCall Paper Doll. Whitman, #4744; 1971. **$4.**

Permission McCall's Publishing Company: Betsy McCall Paper Doll reprinted by permission of
Western Publishing Company, Inc. and McCall's Publishing Company.

Early Barbies, **$10:** *Barbie, Ken, and Midge, Whitman, 1963; Midge, Whitman, 1963; Barbie and Ken Cutouts, Whitman, 1962.*
Reprinted by permission of Western Publishing Company, Inc. ©1962, 1963, Mattel, Inc. Trademarks of Mattel, Inc. used with permission.

1969:

- 1976 Barbie Dolls and Clothes
- 4763 Barbie (box)

1970:

- 510 Barbie Dress Up Kit (Colorforms)
- 1976 Barbie and Ken
- 1981 New 'n Groovy P.J.
- 1985 Barbie and Ken
- 1986 Barbie and Ken

1971:

- 1976 Groovy World of Barbie and Her Friends
- 1981 P.J. Cover Girl Paper Doll
- 1987 World of Barbie
- 4331 Barbie Magic Paper Doll (box)
- 4332 New and Groovy P.J.
- 4735 Barbie Paper Doll (box)

1972:

- 1974 Paper Doll Fashions, Groovy P.J.
- 1975 Paper Doll Fashions P. J. 'n Barbie
- 1994 Malibu Barbie, the Sun Set
- 4343 World of Barbie Play Fun Box
- 4367 World of Barbie
- 4718 Malibu P. J.
- 4376-8 World of Barbie Paper Dolls

1973:

- 1952 Malibu Skipper
- 1954 Barbie's Boutique
- 1955 Malibu Francie
- 1969 Paper Doll Fashions, Hi! I'm Skipper
- 1982 Francie with Growin' Pretty Hair
- 1984 Quick Curl Barbie and Her Paper Doll Friends
- 1990 Barbie Country Camper
- 1996 Barbie's Friendship
- 4322 Barbie's Magic Paper Doll (box)
- 4347 Barbie Country Camper and Paper Doll

1974:

- 920A Barbie Color 'n Play (Colorforms)
- 1951 Barbie Goin' Camping
- 1981 Barbie's Sweet 16!
- 4336 Barbie and Ken—Newport (box)
- 4338 Sun Valley Barbie and Ken

1975:

- 930B Barbie Lace and Dress Dancing Doll (Colorforms)
- 1644 Quick Curl Barbie
- 1956 Yellowstone Kelly
- 1981 Barbie and Her Friends All Sports Tournament
- 2352 Barbie Sport Fashion Set
- 4399 Quick Curl Barbie (box)

1976:

- 1989 Barbie Fashion Originals
- 1990 Growing Up Skipper
- 1996 Barbie's Beach Bus
- 4391 Ballerina Barbie (box)
- 4392 Barbie and Francie (box)
- 4395 Skipper
- 53404 Barbie and Francie
- 4389/7409 Barbie and Ken All Sports Tournament (box)

1977:

- 1983 Superstar Barbie
- 1993 Ballerina Barbie

1978:

- 1982 Fashion Photo Barbie and P. J.
- 74130 Superstar Barbie (box)

1979:

- 1997-21 Fashion Photo Barbie

1980:

- 1836 Barbie and Skipper, Campsite at Lucky Lake (''A Paper Doll Playbook'')
- 1982-31 Starr (Starr, Shawn, Kelly, and Tracey)
- 1982-33 Super Teen Skipper

1981:

- 1836-32 Starr
- 1982-34 Pretty Changes Barbie
- 7408C-21 Skipper and Scott (box)
- 7408D-21 Starr and Shawn

Barbie and psychedelic graphics. Barbie Magic Paper Doll. Whitman, 1971. $2.50.

Barbie Assortment (still on market):
Malibu Barbie, Whitman, 1972;
Barbie Fashion Originals, Whitman, 1976;
Barbie All-Sports Tournament, Whitman, 1975;
Barbie's Boutique, Whitman, 1973.

Ken and Midge costume page. 1963.

Far-out Malibu Barbie costume. Whitman, 1972.
Reprinted by permission of Western Publishing Company, Inc.©1972, Mattel, Inc. Trademarks of Mattel, Inc. used with permission.

Barbie's bicentennial costume. 1976 shirt should endear her to collectors. Barbie's Fashion Originals. Whitman, 1976.
Reprinted by permission of Western Publishing Company, Inc.©1976 Mattel, Inc. Trademarks of Mattel, Inc. used with permission.

III. Now
The Eighties

For the purposes of this book, *now* begins in 1980, a decade that promises wonderful, rich paper dolls. In 1982, it is already apparent that the adult-child paper doll is a popular direction that will be pursued. So far in the 1980s, Dover Publications has released:

More Dolly Dingle (Grace Drayton)
More Lettie Lane (Shelia Young)
Pavlova and Najinsky (Tom Tierney original)
John Wayne (Tom Tierney original)
Vivien Leigh (Tom Tierney original)
Nutcracker Suite Toy Theater (Tom Tierney original)
Carmen Miranda (Tom Tierney original)

And Bellerophon has announced a new paper doll coloring book

John Wayne Paper Dolls by Tom Tierney.
© 1981 Dover Publications, Inc. NY. By permission of Wayne Enterprises.

called The Royal Family. Whitman in 1980 introduced new paper doll books with scenery and settings that are sure to woo a child back to paper doll play. They have even begun a new paper doll series called Star Princess and Pluta, the first space adventure paper dolls for girls.

Probably most fun are the paper dolls of Ronald Reagan. Dell Publishing Company did First Family, by Jim Fitzgerald and John Boswell, with illustrations by Al Kilgore, in 1981. This book includes Ronald, Nancy, the children, and humorous half-figures to cluster about the oval office: Alexander Haig, Brooke Shields, the Carters, an astronaut, and Bonzo. The office contains jelly beans, a Richard Nixon paperweight, and an $8'' \times 10''$ glossy photo of Frank Sinatra inscribed, ''Ron, you did it my way.''

From a company new to paper doll publishing, the Sincere Novelty Company of San Francisco, California, comes a most entertaining series of greeting card paper dolls, beautifully printed and designed by artist David Moore, including The People's Choice, Wife of The People's Choice, and Ronald Reagan, a dancing doll or pantin. These dolls have clever costumes. Future plans of this company include dolls of Lady Di and Charles.

Their royal wedding inspired a wonderful rush of paper doll books. Each is more exciting than the last, and all are infinitely collectible. From England comes The Royal Wedding, published by Courtier Fine Arts Ltd. of London. Simon and Schuster publishes Chuck and Di Have a Baby, by John Boswell, Patty Brown, and Will Elder.

The latter includes the baby in neuter-yellow terries. The baby resembles Winston Churchill and comes complete with a royal nursery, furnished with throned bassinet, regal highchair, wind-up knight in armor, Big Ben, and Eeyor and Tigger in the regal toybox. A cricket match is on the telly. The baby has a Waterford crystal baby bottle, Knight-of-the-Garter teething ring, and an Excalibur good-luck memento. Visitors are Margaret Thatcher, Barbara Cartland, Grandma Queen, Grandpa Duke, and Auntie Anne, with horse.

Perigee Books, an imprint of G. P. Putnam Sons, has produced probably the most beautiful, graceful, and authentic of the books. It is The Princess Diana Paper Doll Book of Fashion, by Clarissa Harlowe and Mary Ann Bedford, with illustrations by Dona Granata. Collectors will want all these books.

Symbolic, perhaps, of something, there has been only one paper doll of a current celebrity movie star or television personality so far in the decade. If, in fact, paper dolls are indicative of the popular period, then the one paper star must be a superior and truly popular person. Of course, she is! She is ''elleself''— Miss Piggy! *

*MISS PIGGY character © Henson Associates, Inc. 1982.

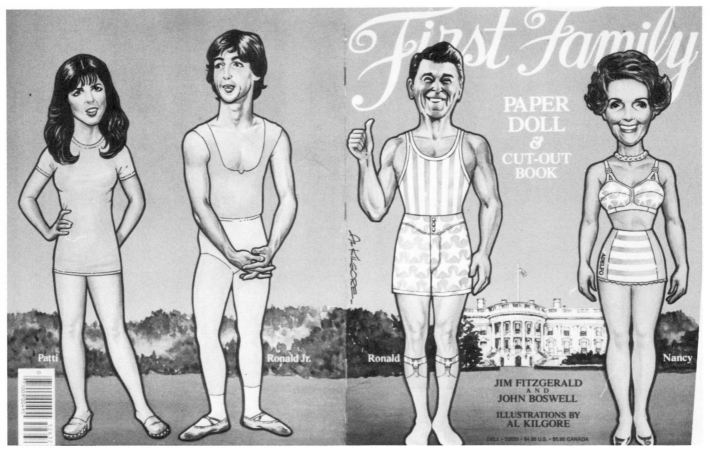

First Family. By Jim Fitzgerald and John Boswell, illustrations by Al Kilgore. ©1981, Dell Publishing.

The People's Choice. Courtesy of David Moore (artist) and Sincere Novelty Company

Ms. Piggy. MISS PIGGY character©Henson Associates, Inc., 1982. Courtesy of Colorforms.

The paper doll future seems bright to me. Contemporary, commercial paper dolls have never been more exciting. They have survived the Barbie blitz and incorporated her into paper. Paper dolls are healthy and strong.

In 1983 there will most likely be an Annie paper doll, since movies advance apace. I hope there is a Kermie, and, perhaps, a preppy doll. Whatever paper dolls are forthcoming, one is sure they will be of high quality, expensive, and fun!

But collectors must worry about handmade-homemade paper dolls from our era. I hope that there are some to hand down to our descendants, and I hope that all collectors are making them. The handmade dolls of the past are great inspirations. Artistic skill is not a requirement. We can do as our ancestors did. We can cut heads from photos, *People Magazine,* or *Time,* and paste them onto bodies, either handmade or cut from *Vogue.*

Scrapbook houses like those of Anita Blair can be a contemporary treasure with solar heating, a Jacuzzi bath, Pepsi, Perrier water, and Rubic's Cube on the coffeetable. Pac-Man must play on the tube, and a Balloons to You Messenger must stand at the door.

Our descendants will find our paper dolls and houses quaint, educational prizes, a great historical record of popular sense and nonsense. Collectors will have a new hobby to pass on to the young. Most of all, the paper doll parade will continue its perspective from the antique through the nostalgic to now. Right on!

Appendix A
Paper Doll Collections

The best way to know, recognize, and love paper dolls is to see them. No photograph can do justice to their beautiful color and texture. Early hand painted commercial paper dolls, both American and European, are truly art, as are the handmade paper dolls of every period. Even the early commercial paper dolls printed in many colors on heavy stock present printing as an everyday fine art, a luxury we cannot economically duplicate today.

Finding paper dolls to see is what is difficult. Unfortunately, paper dolls are often in storage in museums. The museums listed below have paper doll collections. Some are on permanent display. Other museums have collections that are on periodic display or that may be viewed after appointments made in advance. Inquiry at local museums, historical societies, and libraries may disclose one doll or boxes full of dolls that no one has ever asked to see.

I have adopted the following key to collection size:
> *** collections of over 100 sets of paper dolls
> ** collections of about 50 sets of paper dolls
> * small, specialized collections

Paper Dolls on Permanent Display

Maryland:

The Museum and Library of Maryland History in the Maryland Historical Society* 201 West Monument Square, Baltimore, MD 21201
> This museum has, among its collections of rooms, china, glass, and Chesapeake Bay maritime artifacts, which includes the original draft of "The Star Spangled Banner," a small collection of paper dolls on permanent display.

Massachusetts:

The John Greene Chandler Memorial Museum (Little Book House Museum)*** 57 East George Hill Road, South Lancaster, MA 01561
> *Inquiry advised,* as the museum schedule changes with the season. Information from Mr. Herbert Hosmer, Founder and Curator. This charming museum displays important early paper dolls, many of which Hosmer has permitted to be photographed for this book. The museum also displays the paper doll books and paper toys published by John Greene Chandler. Hosmer presents the delightful Toy Cupboard Theater (puppet shows) on a summer schedule and by appointment in winter. Doll houses may be seen by request. A visit to this museum is total enchantment.

Michigan:

Detroit Children's Museum** 67 East Kirby, Detroit, MI 48202
> Has displays of science, folk art, toys, and dolls. Paper dolls are displayed with dolls.

Paper Dolls in Archives Appointments Necessary

Delaware:

The Henry Francis du Pont Winterthur Museum*** Winterthur, DE 19735
> Originally the home of Henry Francis du Pont, the Winterthur Museum and Gardens contains "a collection of collections unique in America." Best described in its own brochure, "the Winterthur is known worldwide. . . . It is an art museum with a matchless collection of antiques made or used in America between 1640 and 1840; it is a historic house museum which offers visitors a sense of the past; it is a garden of great scenic beauty which contains many collections of rare plants while giving the impression of a natural landscape." It is also a research and learning center. The Louise du Pont Crowninshield Research Building is located next to the museum and contains superb library, scientific, and conservation facilities. The magnificent Maxine Waldron paper doll collection, from which many of this book's illustrations come, is housed in the library archives. This collection covers all periods of paper dolls. It is available for researchers. An appointment is necessary.

Illinois:

The Chicago Historical Society** Clark Street at North Avenue, Chicago, IL 60614
> Houses, among its many treasures of Chicago history, an archive of paper dolls. From McLoughlin to Letty Lane, this collection contains a delightful paper doll assortment, including the scrapbooks for Anita Blair. Appointment required.

Indiana:

The Children's Museum** 3000 North Meridian Street, Indianapolis, IN 46208
> The Indianapolis Children's Museum is the largest children's museum in the world. In a handsome modern building situated on five acres of land in central Indianapolis, the museum contains wonders for both child and adult. Best described in the museum's publication *INFO*, the museum "contains treasures on which youthful imaginations thrive—fire engines and trains, dinosaurs and mummies, a cave, a log

cabin, and a carousel to name only a few.'' The museum owns toys, dolls, and a paper doll collection in archive. The dolls are not currently on display, but an advance appointment for research may be made.

Kentucky:

Kentucky Library* Western Kentucky University, Bowling Green, KY 42101

Located on the rolling hills of beautiful Western Kentucky University campus, the Kentucky Library contains a fascinating museum of Kentucky history and a library of special collections, including the Coke Collection of paper dolls. This represents an outstanding representative collection of early American paper doll publishers, including the entire Anson Randolph family. The collection also includes exquisite handmade dolls made by many members of the Coke family.

Massachusetts:

The Essex Institute* 132 Essex Street, Salem, MA 01910

The Essex Institute is a historical museum housing artifacts pertaining to the Houses of Salem. A small, but fascinating, paper doll collection is in archive. Appointment required.

New Jersey:

The New Jersey Historical Society** 230 Broadway, Newark, NJ 07104

This society has in its collections the beautiful unique handmade watercolor paper dolls of Anna Lindner, who was partly crippled by polio during her childhood in Germany. The paper dolls were made in New Jersey between 1860 and 1910. There are at least fifty sets of dolls with over 600 pieces of costume. This is a very special treasure which the museum occasionally incorporates into other exhibits.

The Newark Museum*** 49 Washington Street, Newark, NJ 07101

The Newark Museum has a large representative paper doll collection in storage. This collection has not yet been cataloged, but is available for study and inspection by appointment.

New York:

Ontario County Historical Society* 55 North Main Street, Canadaigua, NY 14975

This society has a few sets of interesting paper dolls, so far uncataloged. These are available to the collector for study by appointment.

De Witt Historical Society* 116 North Cayuga Street, Ithaca, NY 14850

Collection of dolls handmade by Hetty Belle Townley. Dolls in fifty costumes are occasionally on display and may be seen by appointment.

The Cooper-Hewitt Museum* 2 East 91 Street, New York, NY 10028

A small but choice collection of paper dolls, which includes a handmade Jenny Lind. Inquiry and appointment necessary.

The Museum of the City of New York*** Fifth Avenue at 103rd Street, New York, NY 10029

This museum is dedicated to New York history and includes fascinating, fabulous toys, dolls, and doll houses. Paper doll collection from all periods is in archive. Appointment required.

The Margaret Woodbury Strong Museum*** 1 Manhattan Square, Rochester, NY 14607

A history museum, with collections concerning social and cultural northeast America 1820–1930. The museum has an extensive and comprehensive paper doll collection, which is a part of the vast and varied collections of the late Margaret Woodbury Strong. Paper dolls are occasionally on display and may be seen by appointment.

Ohio:

The Kent State University Library*** Kent, OH 44242

The Kent State University Library houses among its important special collections the archives of the Saalfield Company, which includes a major portion of paper dolls published by them from 1930–1960. Available for study and research by appointment.

Pennsylvania:

Chester County Historical Society*** 225 North High Street, Westchester, PA 19380

This museum has a magnificent paper doll collection currently being cataloged by the donor. It is not presently available to the collector.

Vermont:

Shelburne Museum* Shelburne, VT 05482

Among this museum's 35 restored buildings on 100 acres of land is a toy museum, which houses a small, but interesting, paper doll collection in archive. By appointment.

Appendix B Books and Newsletters

Books

Just as no one collector can collect every paper doll, no one book can contain all paper doll information. Serious collectors need libraries, and the books recommended here are currently in print.

Howard, Marian B. *Those Fascinating Paper Dolls: An Illustrated Handbook for Collectors.* New York: Dover Publications, 1981.

Jendrick, Barbara Whitton. *A Picture Book of Paper Dolls and Paper Toys.* 1974. (Available from Paper Soldier. See Appendix E.)

Krebs, Martha K. *Advertising Paper Dolls: A Guide for Collectors,* Vols. I and II. 1975. (Available from author, 13628 Middlevale Lane, Silver Spring, MD 20906, $8 each, $15 both.)

Young, Mary. *Paper Dolls and Their Artists,* Vol. I, 1975, Vol. II, 1977. (Available from Paper Soldier or Paul Ruddell. See Appendix E.)

Young, Mary. *A Collector's Guide to Paper Dolls: Saalfield, Lowe, and Merrill.* Puducah, Kentucky: Collector's Books, 1980.

Woodcock, Jean. *Paper Dolls of Famous Faces,* Vol. II. Cumberland, Maryland: Hobby House Press, 1980.

Newsletters

Celebrity Doll Journal. Loraine Burdick, 5 Court Place, Puyaleep, WA 98371 (Covers dolls, artists, toys, and paper dolls.)

Matchmaker. Fran Van Vynckt, 6931 Monroe Avenue, Hammond, IN 46324 (Dedicated to helping find bits and pieces of incomplete sets. Six issues a year.)

Midwest Paper Dolls and Toys Quarterly. Janie Varsolona, Box 131, Galesburg, KA 66740 (Four issues a year.)

Paper Doll Gazette. Shirley Hedge, Route 2, Princeton, IN 47670 (Five issues.)

Paper Playthings. Joan Carol Kaltschmidt, 7519 162nd Street, Flushing, NY 11365

Appendix C
Preservation, Framing, and Storage

Paper

Paper has been known since 105 A.D. It is believed to have been first produced in China. Early paper contained a high content of cotton and linen fiber, and much paper was made by mills using water hard with limestone. The paper produced was exceptionally durable, and early paper dolls, such as the English toy books and the imported boxed European paper dolls, were made from this fine paper. This fact helps explain the remarkable, fresh appearance these antique paper dolls have today.

In 1843, Frederick Keller of Germany began producing wood pulp paper. By 1870, wood pulp paper was used almost exclusively. Naturally. It was a cheaper process and wood was abundant. However, with the introduction of wood pulp, the problems of paper deterioration began, and this is a problem that all paper doll collectors must consider.

Storage

Aging paper creates an acid, and acid is the great paper destroyer and enemy. Cherished, valuable paper dolls should be kept in acid-free storage. There are many options available to collectors for this type of storage, and supplies may be purchased from library or genealogy supply stores.

In general, it is supposed that the collector desires see-through storage in order to view dolls. Mylar is the best clear material to surround a paper doll with. It is sold in sheets and may be made into folders for paper dolls. It is expensive. Polyester sheets are considered by paper experts to be almost as fine as mylar for display and storage purposes, and it is a cheaper material. Gene-alogy stores carry this material as Poly C. Acid-free bags are another option for the collector. Once again, library and gene-alogy stores carry this merchandise.

Albums

Most collectors use albums to store cut paper dolls. The magnetic type is easy to use, but paper dolls should not come in contact with the gummy substance used as a packing for photographs. Collectors should insert a piece of acid-free mylar or Poly C paper between the doll and the album backing, and another piece of the same material between the front of the doll and the clear sheet of the album. (The acid-free sheets, of course, should be smaller than the enclosing sheet of the album, so there will be enough album front left to close and seal the doll into the book.)

Framing

Paper dolls are interesting when framed. Once again, paper preservation should be considered, and the doll should be framed against an acid-free backing, mylar, Poly C, or a de-acidified material. A commercial spray solution, Weit'o, is available to accomplish de-acidification. It, too, is found at library and genealogical supply stores.

Paper dolls should never be attached to backing with anything other than a stamp hinge (sold in stamp hobby stores), as tapes and press-ons scar paper dolls.

Source

Should you not have a supply store in your area, supplies may be found by writing to **TALAS** (Technical Library Service) 104 Fifth Avenue, New York, NY 10011.

Appendix D
Paper Doll Print Terminology

Woodcut A printing method used since the fifteenth century for printing books. Wood is chiseled away from the design, leaving the design in relief. The ink is applied to the relief, and the impression is then made.

Wood engraving A refinement of the woodblock developed in the last half of the eighteenth century in England by Thomas Bewick and used by McLoughlin Brothers and other early printers of paper dolls. In this method, the artist cuts a hardwood block of boxwood with an engraver's tool, the burin, to make the design, and an engraver does the relief cutting. This permits a fine design to be made easily by the artist.

Engraving An early printing method used, for example, for pantins. Lines are incised on copper or steel and inked over. The impression is then made from the metal plates.

Lithograph Printing is done from lines drawn upon stone (limestone) with a greasy crayon. The stone is wet with water and inked. The ink adheres only to the crayon, and thus the impression is made when applied to paper. Discovered by Alois Senefelder in Germany in 1798, this method was used for paper doll printing until photographic methods of printing took over.

Pochoir A French term describing the early method of coloring black and white prints, illustrations, and paper dolls. Color is skillfully applied by hand stencil to engraved, woodcut or lithographed dolls.

Chromolithography "Chromos" were very popular colored lithographed prints sold in the latter part of the 1800s. The method used involved several lithographic stones applied to the same print, thus producing a color print. This method was used for making paper dolls until photographic methods were developed.

Appendix E
Doll Sources

Paper dolls may be obtained by mail from the following:

Bellerophon Books 36 Anacapa Street, Santa Barbara, CA 93101
>   Catalog available on request.

Dealer-Collector paper doll lists in newsletters (see Appendix B)

Dover Publications 180 Varick Street, New York, NY 10014
>   Catalog available on request, free of charge. It is a good idea to mention specific interest, since Dover has many catalogs for different areas. Paper dolls may be ordered.

Paper Soldier 8 McIntosh Lane, Clifton Park, NY 12065
>   Carries a large assortment of difficult-to-find paper dolls and paper doll books. Catalog $2. Paper dolls and books sent by mail.

Paul Ruddell 900 Frederick Street, Cumberland, MD 21502
>   Books on hobbies for collectors. Carries paper dolls and collector books. Catalog for mail order.

Bibliography

Books

Ackley, Edith Flack. *Paper Dolls: Their History and How to Make Them.* New York: Frederic A. Stokes Co., 1939.

American Heritage Publishing Co. "The Twenties," *American Heritage* 16 (1965): special issue.

Blum, Stella. *Victorian Fashions and Costumes: "Harper's Bazaar" 1897–1898.* New York: Dover Publications, 1974.

Crouse, Russel. *Mr. Currier and Mr. Ives.* New York: Garden City Publishing Co., Inc., 1930.

Howard, Marian B. *Those Fascinating Paper Dolls: An Illustrated Handbook for Collectors.* New York: Dover Publications, 1981.

Jendrick, Barbara Whitton. *Paper Dolls and Paper Toys of Raphael Tuck and Sons.* Barbara Whitton Jendrick, 1970.

King, Constance Eileen. *The Encyclopedia of Toys.* New York: Crown, 1978.

King, Constance Eileen. *The Collector's History of Dolls.* New York: Bonanza Books, 1977.

Mayer, Ralph. *A Dictionary of Art Terms and Techniques.* New York: Thomas Y. Crowell Co., 1969.

McClellan, Elizabeth. *History of American Costume 1607–1870.* New York: Tudor Publishing Co., 1937.

McClinton, Katharine Morrison. *Antiques of American Childhood.* New York: Bramhall House, 1970.

National Geographic Society. *We Americans.* Washington, D.C.: National Geographic Society, 1975.

Rogers, Agnes. *Women Are Here to Stay.* New York: Harper Brothers Publishers, 1949.

Sezan, Claude. *Les Poupees Anciennes.* Editions Pittoresques. Paris, France: Paris Les Editions, 1930.

Schiller, Justin G. and Wagner, Raymond M. *Catalogue 35: Original Wood Blocks from the Archives of McLoughlin Brothers.* New York: Justin G. Schiller Ltd., 1978.

Von Boehn, Max. *Dolls and Puppets.* London: George G. Harrap and Co., Ltd., 1932.

Woodcock, Jean. *Paper Dolls of Famous Faces. Vol. I.* New York: Jean Woodcock, 1974.

Woodcock, Jean. *Paper Dolls of Famous Faces. Vol. II.* Cumberland, Maryland: Hobby House Press, 1980.

Young, Mary. *Paper Dolls and Their Artists. Vol. I.* Mary Young, 1975.

Young, Mary. *Paper Dolls and Their Artists. Vol. II. Mary Young, 1977.*

Young, Mary. A Collector's Guide to Paper Dolls: Saalfield, Lowe and Merrill. Puducah, Kentucky: Collector Books, 1980.

Periodicals

Wingate, Robert Bray. "Restoring Old Books," *Early American Life,* December, 1977.

Index